CAMBRIDGE
UNIVERSITY PRESS

CAMBRIDGE ENGLISH
Language Assessment
Part of the University of Cambridge

Cambridge English

CAMBRIDGE OFFICIAL PREPARATION MATERIAL

FIRST for Schools 3

WITHOUT ANSWERS

AUTHENTIC EXAMINATION PAPERS

Cambridge University Press
www.cambridge.org/elt

Cambridge Assessment English
www.cambridgeenglish.org

Information on this title: www.cambridge.org/9781108433761

First published 2018

20 19 18 17 16 15 14 13

Printed in Great Britain by CPI Group (UK) Ltd, Croydon CR0 4YY

A catalogue record for this publication is available from the British Library

ISBN 978-1-108-43378-5 Student's Book with answers
ISBN 978-1-108-38085-0 Student's Book with answers with Audio
ISBN 978-1-108-43376-1 Student's Book without answers
ISBN 978-1-108-43381-5 Audio CDs (2)

Contents

Introduction

This collection of four complete practice tests comprises papers from the *Cambridge English: First for Schools* examination; students can practise these tests on their own or with the help of a teacher.

The *Cambridge English: First for Schools* examination is part of a suite of general English examinations produced by Cambridge English Language Assessment. This suite consists of five examinations that have similar characteristics but are designed for different levels of English language ability. Within the five levels, *Cambridge English: First for Schools* is at Level B2 in the Council of Europe's *Common European Framework of Reference for Languages: Learning, teaching, assessment*. It has been accredited by Ofqual, the statutory regulatory authority in England, at Level 1 in the National Qualifications Framework. The *Cambridge English: First for Schools* examination is widely recognised in commerce and industry and in individual university faculties and other educational institutions.

Examination	Council of Europe Framework Level	UK National Qualifications Framework Level
Cambridge English: Proficiency *Certificate of Proficiency in English (CPE)*	C2	3
Cambridge English: Advanced *Certificate in Advanced English (CAE)*	C1	2
Cambridge English: First for Schools *First Certificate in English (FCE) for Schools*	B2	1
Cambridge English: Preliminary *Preliminary English Test (PET)*	B1	Entry 3
Cambridge English: Key *Key English Test (KET)*	A2	Entry 2

Cambridge English: First for Schools follows the same format as *Cambridge English: First* and the level of the question papers is identical. The only difference is that the content and treatment of topics in *Cambridge English: First for Schools* have been particularly targeted at the interest and experience of school pupils. *Cambridge English: First for Schools* candidates who achieve Grade C or higher in the exam receive a *Cambridge English: First for Schools* certificate.

Further information

The information contained in this practice book is designed to be an overview of the exam. For a full description of all of the above exams, including information about task types, testing focus and preparation, please see the relevant handbooks which can be obtained from Cambridge English Language Assessment at the address below or from the website at: www.cambridgeenglish.org

Cambridge English Language Assessment
1 Hills Road
Cambridge CB1 2EU
United Kingdom

Telephone: +44 1223 553997
Email: helpdesk@cambridgeenglish.org

The structure of *Cambridge English: First for Schools*: an overview

The *Cambridge English: First for Schools* examination consists of four papers.

Reading and Use of English 1 hour 15 minutes
This paper consists of **seven parts**, with 52 questions. For Parts 1 to 4, the test contains texts with accompanying grammar and vocabulary tasks, and separate items with a grammar and vocabulary focus. For Parts 5 to 7, the test contains a range of texts and accompanying reading comprehension tasks.

Writing 1 hour 20 minutes
This paper consists of **two parts** which carry equal marks. In Part 1, which is **compulsory**, candidates have to write an essay of between 140 and 190 words, giving their opinion in response to a task. In Part 2, there are four tasks from which candidates **choose one** to write about. The range of tasks from which questions may be drawn includes an article, an email/letter, an essay, a review and a short story. The last question is based on a set text. In this part, candidates have to write between 140 and 190 words.

Listening 40 minutes (approximately)
This paper consists of **four parts.** Each part contains a recorded text or texts and some questions, including multiple-choice, sentence completion and multiple-matching. Each text is heard twice. There is a total of **30 questions.**

Speaking 14 minutes
The Speaking test consists of **four parts.** The standard test format is two candidates and two examiners. One examiner takes part in the conversation while the other examiner listens. Both examiners give marks. Candidates will be given photographs and other visual and written materials to look at and talk about. Sometimes candidates will talk with the other candidate, sometimes with the examiner, and sometimes with both.

Grading

Candidates will receive a score on the Cambridge English Scale for each of the four skills and Use of English. The average of these five scores gives the candidate's overall Cambridge English Scale score for the exam. This determines what grade and CEFR level they achieve. All candidates receive a Statement of Results and candidates who pass the examination with Grade A, B or C also receive the *First Certificate in English*. Candidates who achieve Grade A receive the *First Certificate in English* stating that they demonstrated ability at Level C1. Candidates who achieve Grade B or C receive the *First Certificate in English* certificate stating that they demonstrated ability at Level B2. Candidates whose performance is below B2 level, but falls within Level B1, receive a *Cambridge English* certificate stating that they have demonstrated ability at Level B1. Candidates whose performance falls below Level B1 do not receive a certificate.

For further information on grading and results, go to the website (see page 5).

Test 1

READING AND USE OF ENGLISH (1 hour 15 minutes)

Part 1

For questions **1–8**, read the text below and decide which answer (**A**, **B**, **C** or **D**) best fits each gap. There is an example at the beginning (**0**).

Mark your answers **on the separate answer sheet.**

Example:

0 **A** describes **B** suggests **C** explains **D** shows

0	A	B	C	D
	▭	▬	▭	▭

Chocolate teapots really are useful

A chocolate teapot is not as useless as the old British saying **(0)** .... Scientists have shown it's possible to use one to make tea. They've created a chocolate teapot that can be filled with boiling water and left to **(1)** .... for two minutes, after which the tea is ready to be served.

After **(2)** .... a range of experiments, the scientists **(3)** .... to the conclusion that the **(4)** .... to making a teapot that wouldn't melt was to use dark chocolate with 65% chocolate solids and build up a series of layers to strengthen it. This whole process took around two-and-a-half hours.

At first the scientists wondered whether they might **(5)** .... end up with chocolate tea. They discovered some of the chocolate on the inside of the pot would melt, but **(6)** .... that the water was poured in carefully, the **(7)** .... majority of it wouldn't be affected. When they tried the tea, the team agreed it was lovely with a **(8)** .... taste of chocolate.

1	**A**	hold	**B**	keep	**C**	stand	**D**	wait
2	**A**	investigating	**B**	conducting	**C**	researching	**D**	exploring
3	**A**	arrived	**B**	reached	**C**	drew	**D**	came
4	**A**	secret	**B**	clue	**C**	method	**D**	formula
5	**A**	again	**B**	still	**C**	clearly	**D**	simply
6	**A**	allowed	**B**	considered	**C**	provided	**D**	assumed
7	**A**	huge	**B**	broad	**C**	high	**D**	vast
8	**A**	modest	**B**	slight	**C**	soft	**D**	gentle

Part 2

For questions **9–16**, read the text below and think of the word which best fits each gap. Use only **one** word in each gap. There is an example at the beginning (**0**).

Write your answers **IN CAPITAL LETTERS on the separate answer sheet**.

Example: | 0 | | H | A | V | E |

Making mistakes helps you to succeed

(0) .... you ever tried a new sport or learnt to play a musical instrument? **(9)** .... so, you'll know that once you figure **(10)** .... how to do it and get good at it, you won't lose your skills, even when you haven't practised for a long time. Most experts put this down to 'muscle memory', which means the brain remembers an action and can recall it when needed. Now some researchers believe there's another important factor: errors that occur while learning a task.

(11) .... surprised the researchers is that getting things wrong not only trains the brain to perform better at a specific task, but also helps it to learn faster. This is true even when mistakes are **(12)** .... while learning a completely new task. The researchers believe that the brain keeps a record **(13)** .... errors and draws on them whenever a new skill **(14)** .... being learnt. This ensures that mistakes aren't repeated, and probably explains why people **(15)** .... master one sport or instrument can pick **(16)** .... others with relative ease.

Part 3

For questions **17–24**, read the text below. Use the word given in capitals at the end of some of the lines to form a word that fits in the gap **in the same line**. There is an example at the beginning (**0**).

Write your answers **IN CAPITAL LETTERS on the separate answer sheet.**

Example: | 0 | A M A Z I N G |

Have a go at kayaking

I've discovered an **(0)** .... sport: kayaking. It looks very	**AMAZE**
(17) .... when you see it on TV, and apparently it's been increasing in	**IMPRESS**
(18) .... over the past few years. I'm not actually a very sporty	**POPULAR**
person but when my sister, a keen kayaker herself, bought me a lesson	
for my birthday that was my opportunity to have a go.	
It was a **(19)** .... to discover I wasn't the only beginner – everyone	**RELIEVE**
else was also very **(20)** .... like me. At first we were all pretty	**EXPERIENCE**
(21) .... and some of us even fell in the water, but we learnt quickly	**HOPE**
and our confidence began to grow.	
I loved being on the river. The **(22)** .... were so beautiful and	**SURROUND**
relaxing that I was really reluctant to get out of the kayak when	
the lesson finished! It was a truly **(23)** .... day. I signed up for a	**MEMORY**
one-week course without a moment's hesitation. Now I'm just as	
(24) .... about kayaking as my sister.	**PASSION**

Part 4

For questions **25–30**, complete the second sentence so that it has a similar meaning to the first sentence, using the word given. **Do not change the word given**. You must use between **two** and **five** words, including the word given. Here is an example (**0**).

Example:

0 Prizes are given out when the school year finishes.

PLACE

Prize-giving .... end of the school year.

The gap can be filled by the words 'takes place at the', so you write:

Example:

0	*TAKES PLACE AT THE*

Write **only** the missing words **IN CAPITAL LETTERS on the separate answer sheet.**

---

25 Seeing Pete sitting in the café was a real surprise.

EXPECTED

I really .... Pete sitting in the café.

26 My aunt said we could stay at her house for a few nights during the holidays.

PUT

My aunt said she could .... at her house for a few nights during the holidays.

27 Anne says she doesn't want to make the effort to tidy her room, even though it's a mess!

BOTHERED

Anne says she .... to tidy her room, even though it's a mess!

28 Could you look after my little brother for a minute, please?

EYE

Could you .... my little brother for a minute, please?

29 Jo's mother told her that it wasn't a good idea to eat so many biscuits before lunch!

DISCOURAGE

Jo's mother tried .... so many biscuits before lunch!

30 The teacher didn't think about the fact that it might rain when she planned the school trip.

ACCOUNT

The teacher failed .... the fact that it might rain when she planned the school trip.

Part 5

You are going to read an extract from an interview with a young novelist. For questions **31–36**, choose the answer (**A**, **B**, **C** or **D**) which you think fits best according to the text.

Mark your answers **on the separate answer sheet.**

Young writer

Charlotte Grainger explains that it was her primary school teacher who first speculated that she might write a novel. 'I thought the height of achievement would be to write a book because it seemed such a challenge and anyway I didn't know what other teenagers were doing, like being in the Olympics, for example. When I turned 13 I thought: "I may as well attempt this now".' The novel Charlotte started then is, remarkably, about to be published. 'Recently I told my ex-teacher about it and she was astonished. She told me she'd meant I'd probably do it when I was 30 or 40. That had never occurred to me – I couldn't understand why I'd be expected to put something on hold that I had a chance of being good at.'

It's a winter afternoon, in the offices of Charlotte's publishers. Even though I knew that I was going to interview a 15-year-old girl about her book, I was still momentarily thrown by seeing a teenager sitting there. The book is a huge achievement: the narrative is assured and action packed. Nothing about it, except the age of its heroine, suggests that it was written by a teenager. The public relations representative for the book is keeping us company in case Charlotte might need defending. But she needs neither parental nor professional support. She's her own person: spirited, with an alert face and a lively intelligence, but also a steadiness that prevents any overconfidence she could be forgiven for feeling.

I ask her about the sophisticated moral issues she raises. 'I was trying to ask big questions, not answer them. There aren't many life lessons I can pass on to my readers,' she responds, laughing. 'I don't think my understanding of the world is limited by my age, but neither do I believe I'm particularly wise. I was just interested in exploring the theme of taking responsibility.'

She has a theory about teenagers and the way they are 'betrayed' by the fiction that is specifically aimed at them. There are, she maintains, three types of teenager depicted in novels. 'There's the outsider who becomes acceptable to society, the naïve teenager who knows nothing about the big wide world, and the awkward teenage character who isn't socially skilled.' Repeatedly reading about these character types irritated her. 'What if you're basically fine? There aren't many stories out there about characters who aren't inadequate in some way. The overall impression teenagers can get from some writers – and I don't think it's intentional – is teenagers can't possibly know who they are because they're not experienced enough to know the truth. And when that *line 58*
is being pushed on them by writers, it can undermine their self-belief'.

Charlotte has always been a keen reader of famous fantasy writers, some of whom you might suppose she'd be indebted to, but in fact they almost put her off writing entirely. 'Books by my favourite fantasy writers explore deep things about psychology and about life. I was asking myself: is this seriously what I have to be doing to write a good book and am I really up to it?' She does, however, praise the influence of a book called *How Not to Write a Novel*. 'It tells you that if the reader starts to guess what's going to happen, the suspense has probably gone.'

It would be easy to argue that Charlotte's parents both being journalists was the decisive factor in getting her novel published. Indeed, her father's acquaintance with someone in publishing was what got her book read initially. She acknowledges her good fortune, because getting anyone to read a first novel is hard, whatever the age of the author. 'Every aspiring writer needs support and a lucky break, but after that you're on your own. Ultimately writers sink or swim according to their talents so I don't take things for granted,' Charlotte concludes.

31 Charlotte says she wrote her first novel when she was only 13 because

A she thought it was the easiest way to achieve something great.
B she found it impossible to imagine that delaying was an option.
C she was determined to prove that age was no barrier to success.
D she wanted to live up to her teacher's high expectations of her.

32 What does the writer say about Charlotte in the second paragraph?

A She should take more advice from others.
B She is more modest than might be expected.
C She is more confident in her abilities than she should be.
D She should be allowed more independence.

33 What does Charlotte feel about the characters in teenage fiction?

A They are people who lack confidence or self-awareness.
B They are people with qualities that aren't believable.
C They are created by writers with no interest in young people.
D They are people that readers can identify with easily.

34 What does 'that' refer to in line 58?

A a criticism of how teenagers behave
B the harsh reality of everyday life for teenagers
C an alternative viewpoint for teenagers to consider
D an assumption about the nature of teenagers

35 What was Charlotte's attitude to the famous writers she read?

A She was pleased that they dealt with topics she was interested in.
B She was disappointed by the predictable nature of some stories.
C She became aware of how challenging it would be to write in a similar way.
D She became conscious of the way they had stimulated her imagination.

36 How does she feel about her experience of writing?

A She is annoyed that people focus on how fortunate she has been.
B She regrets that she may have to depend on others.
C She accepts that her early success may not continue.
D She doubts that people fully appreciate her talent.

Part 6

You are going to read a newspaper article about research on the effect of light on students. Six sentences have been removed from the article. Choose from the sentences **A–G** the one which fits each gap (**37–42**). There is one extra sentence which you do not need to use.

Mark your answers **on the separate answer sheet.**

Lighting up the winter darkness

In northern Scandinavia the long dark winters can be difficult. The students in Dragonskolan, a secondary school in Umeå, in Sweden's far north, are taking part in an experiment to see whether using intense electric light, known as 'full-spectrum' light, can help with this problem. This light is much brighter than the lighting currently used in most schools and homes.

This experiment is also part of a bigger debate about using full-spectrum light in schools to relieve tiredness and lack of energy. These symptoms can develop when sleep patterns are disturbed by the very long nights. **37** ______ It is not unusual, for example, for some students to fall asleep on the journey to school.

But last month Dragonskolan school installed 140 full-spectrum lamps in several classrooms. Now, stepping through the door in the morning is like walking into bright sunshine. Students even find themselves glancing out of the window, surprised to see that the sun hasn't come up yet. **38** ______

The school is the first to use this simple technique to try to improve students' performance. Light tells the brain to halt production of melatonin – the hormone that makes you sleepy. **39** ______ Researcher Dr Mariana Figueiro believes that, during the winter, the effects of the lack of light can slowly build up and make your 'body clock' confused. Exposure to light of the correct wavelength and intensity helps the body to know when to switch off in the evening. So you sleep more and feel better the next morning.

40 ______ When a sleep researcher at Stockholm told a conference of head teachers about the benefits of installing full-spectrum lights, they objected, saying that pupils would become restless and be unable to concentrate on their work. Money was also a concern for them because some schools didn't have the budget for these lights.

But those like Figueiro, who are arguing for change, point to other evidence to support their case. **41** ______ Designers may have ignored the significance of this, as giving any consideration to light in their designs seems to have become too low a priority.

For all these reasons, it's not surprising that only a few head teachers have experimented with the lighting in their schools. At Dragonskolan, head teacher Stellan Andersson initially understood this reluctance. After all, some studies suggested that although people claimed the brighter lights were having a positive effect on them, there was no measurable evidence to support this. Equally though, there was no evidence that they actually caused any harm. **42** ______ So Andersson decided to go ahead with installing them hoping for better academic performance. But, whether this happens or not, the students are certainly enjoying the bright new teaching environment.

A Without that stimulus, the body delays, by a few minutes every day, the signal that it's time to wake up.

B What's more, it seems that sitting in a brightly lit room could help people cope with this.

C In fact, there's a much more positive atmosphere there these days.

D Light was once a vital consideration in the planning of school buildings, with books written as far back as the late 19th century focusing on the importance of daylight in the classroom.

E Many in this part of the country freely admit how difficult it is to get ready for the day ahead, several hours before the sun comes up.

F However, despite the apparent simplicity of the theory, little research has been done on the effects of light in schools, so not all of them are keen to change their lighting systems.

G Therefore, it seemed on the face of it that there was nothing to lose.

Part 7

You are going to read five reviews of songs by teenage boy bands. For questions **43–52,** choose from the reviews (**A–E**). The reviews may be chosen more than once.

Mark your answers **on the separate answer sheet**.

Which review

mentions that the song was the best the band released?	**43**	
says the song's lyrics are surprisingly effective when performed?	**44**	
says some instruments cannot be clearly heard?	**45**	
says the song has wide appeal despite its style?	**46**	
suggests the track deserved to have been appreciated more?	**47**	
says that the track has not lost any of its originality?	**48**	
mentions an opportunity for everyone in the band to display their singing ability?	**49**	
mentions the influence someone outside the band had on its music?	**50**	
says that the song is easy to relate to?	**51**	
admires a voice that is not what it seems?	**52**	

Reviews of songs by teenage boy bands

A *Fran*, by The Warts

A significant problem faced by boy bands is the narrow musical range expected of them. On the one hand, there's pop-rock, on the other, a dull version of rhythm and blues. Anything that differs from those styles sounds wildly creative, which may explain the phenomenal success of The Wart's hit song *Fran* in the music charts. The keyboard plays a central role on this track, giving it a sad feel. The lyrics are cleverly written, with each song-line starting with the last word of the previous line. This is more impressive than you might think just reading about it, because each band member takes a line in turn. It's a showcase for The Warts' excellent voices, and lead singer Mike Royce is outstanding.

B *Hard Shell*, by Loud

Loud specialised in disco music until three years ago, when a new producer was brought in who gave them a completely different sound. This has resulted in a string of recent hits although their latest song, *Hard Shell*, is heavy with electronic synthesizers, string instruments and horns. Ned Laing leads on vocals, guitarist Grant Berry manages a creditable solo, and the band's rhythm section is faultless. But at just two-and-a-half minutes long, it's over before you know it. And sadly, the song lacks the memorable lyrics of their earlier successes. In the end, it seems to have proved too polished for their younger fans, and too lightweight for the older ones. It hasn't been a hit, though many in the industry feel it should have been.

C *What I Lost*, by Dealt

Though Dealt got together to compete with other popular boy bands, their first single, *What I Lost*, had few of the elements that defined boy band music at the time: none of the sophisticated disco beats that might have been expected. Instead, it's understated rhythm and blues with a trace of folk, and accented by that least cool of instruments, the accordion. It was a fantastic debut; four years later, it's still unique, as different from the usual boy-band style as accordions are from electronic synthesisers, though both were used on the song. And although the subject matter, romance, is familiar, there's a clever twist: *What I Lost* is set in a courtroom. It was a track that was hard to improve on, and they never did.

D *No Grace*, by the Bowls

Boy band The Bowls' hit song *No Grace* features Len Blane's gentle lead vocals and flowing harmonies from some of the other band members. Say what you like about Blane, but there's no doubt that he has a gift for writing poetic love songs and arranging them to music. *No Grace*, which he claims to have written in an afternoon, is one of his finest songs. It's become a classic guilty pleasure for many people who wouldn't normally admit to liking a soft-pop love song – but why feel guilty? There's something touching about the lyrics and they deal with themes that everyone will have experienced at some time in their lives.

E *Floss*, by Slog

Released while Slog were at their short-lived peak, their hit song *Floss* is a splendid example of attitude plus technology. It opens with a drum solo, which gives way to three minutes of keyboard craziness that sounds like something a far more experimental band might have come up with. The three Slog members play conventional guitars and drums, but it's virtually impossible to detect them over the unusual electronic sounds of the backing track. Then there's lead singer Mo Aramba's remarkable vocals – more those of a thirty-year-old, than of a boy of seventeen. *Floss* is a marvellous track, and an inspiration for boy bands everywhere.

WRITING (1 hour 20 minutes)

Part 1

You **must** answer this question. Write your answer in **140–190** words in an appropriate style **on the separate answer sheet**.

---

1 In your English class you have been talking about decisions which teenagers sometimes have to make. Now your English teacher has asked you to write an essay for homework.

Write your essay using **all** the notes and giving reasons for your point of view.

Is it better for teenagers to make their own decisions or to ask for advice from other people?

Notes

Write about:

1. deciding which subjects to study
2. choosing clothes
3. .... (your own idea)

Part 2

Write an answer to **one** of the questions **2–4** in this part. Write your answer in **140–190** words in an appropriate style **on the separate answer sheet**. Put the question number in the box at the top of the answer sheet.

---

2 You see this announcement in an international e-magazine about the environment:

> *Articles wanted*
>
> **Inventions and the environment**
>
> In your opinion, which invention has had a good effect on the environment and which invention has had a bad effect? Why?
>
> The best articles will appear online next week.

Write your **article**.

3 You have received this email from your English friend, Naomi:

> Hi – my family's moving house next month. I know you moved house recently, too, so do you have any advice for me? I'm also a bit worried about living in a new area and making new friends.
> Have you got any suggestions?
>
> Thanks
>
> Naomi

Write your **email**.

4 You have seen this announcement in a new English-language magazine for schools:

> **Stories wanted**
>
> We are looking for stories for our new English-language magazine for teenagers. Your story must **begin** with this sentence:
>
> *Jess opened the envelope, wondering who it could be from.*
>
> Your story must include:
> - an invitation
> - a surprise

Write your **story**.

LISTENING (approximately 40 minutes)

Part 1

You will hear people talking in eight different situations.

For questions **1–8**, choose the best answer (**A**, **B** or **C**).

---

1 You hear a singer talking about performing on stage.

What does she do if she feels nervous before a performance?

A She pretends the audience is not there.

B She talks with other people in her group.

C She uses a technique suggested by a colleague.

2 You hear a girl telling her father about a special day at school.

How did she feel?

A surprised to be asked for her views

B excited about meeting someone well known

C pleased that her talents were recognised

3 You hear two friends talking about a summer camp they could both go on.

What would they both find difficult about going on it?

A being away from home

B getting on with other people

C doing the organised activities

4 You hear a boy talking about his favourite TV programme.

How does he feel about it?

A disappointed by the absence of one important element

B surprised by the references to real historical figures

C confused by the way the characters behave

5 You hear a journalist talking about an unusual type of house.

What does he think of it?

A He's impressed by how original the design is.

B He's confident that it could be successful elsewhere.

C He's keen to experience staying in it himself.

6 You hear part of an interview with a boy called Max, who found a prehistoric object.

What effect has the discovery had on Max's life?

A It's made him more confident.

B It's provided him with a new interest.

C It's changed the way his friends treat him.

7 You hear a girl talking about the sport called netball.

What does she say about it?

A The rules are quite complicated.

B The skills are difficult to acquire.

C The level of fitness needed is surprising.

8 You hear two friends discussing a news story about some rock climbers.

How does the boy feel about it?

A He feels sorry for the families of the climbers.

B He admires the courage the climbers showed.

C He's determined to follow the climbers' example.

Part 2

You will hear a woman called Ingrid talking about doing volunteer work on a shark conservation project on the island of Fiji. For questions **9–18**, complete the sentences with a word or short phrase.

Shark conservation project on Fiji

Ingrid first came across information about the shark project in a **(9)** .... report.

Ingrid was taught how to dive in a **(10)** .... near her home.

Ingrid says she'll never forget the **(11)** .... on the day she arrived in Fiji.

Ingrid uses the word **(12)** .... to describe her experience of seeing sharks while diving.

Ingrid says that the **(13)** .... of the Bull Sharks was what impressed her most.

Ingrid was pleased to be able to dive to a depth of **(14)** .... metres.

Ingrid mainly worked with researchers who were collecting information about the shark **(15)** .... in the local area.

Ingrid helped researchers to attach metal tags to **(16)** .... Bull Sharks in order to track where they go.

Ingrid was disappointed that she never saw a **(17)** .... Shark.

Ingrid has kept in touch with someone from **(18)** .... , who she met on the project.

Part 3

You will hear five short extracts in which teenagers are talking about their experience of doing experiments in science lessons at school. For questions **19–23**, choose from the list (**A–H**) how each speaker feels about their experience. Use the letters only once. There are three extra letters which you do not need to use.

A bored by having to do things many times

B proud of their ability to be adaptable

C frustrated that important work had to be done too quickly

D inspired by the feedback that was given

E embarrassed by the mistakes that were made

F relieved that the results were better than expected

G disappointed by the lack of support from the teacher

H irritated by someone's lack of organisation

Speaker 1		**19**
Speaker 2		**20**
Speaker 3		**21**
Speaker 4		**22**
Speaker 5		**23**

Part 4

You will hear an interview with an air traffic controller called Jake Watson, whose job involves directing aircraft in and out of an airport. For questions **24–30**, choose the best answer (**A**, **B** or **C**).

---

24 What does Jake find most challenging about his job?

A communicating with a variety of people

B focusing on several tasks at the same time

C being responsible for aircraft safety

25 Why did Jake decide to become an air traffic controller?

A He hoped to increase his income.

B He felt the need to do something different.

C He was unable to fulfil his dream of becoming a commercial pilot.

26 Jake says the selection process for the job showed him that

A he was stronger in some skills than he'd thought.

B he'd be able to develop skills he already had.

C he needed to learn a number of new skills.

27 Jake says the first time he worked without supervision, he

A wished he was still being monitored.

B felt completely ready to deal with it.

C was too busy to let it worry him at all.

28 Jake says that when no planes are flying due to fog, controllers

A use equipment to assess possible solutions to the problem.

B work harder than usual to monitor changing conditions.

C take advantage of a break from their normal routine.

29 What does Jake say about flight delays?

A He finds them irritating when he's a passenger himself.

B He avoids thinking about passengers' problems when he's working.

C He thinks passengers should be given clearer information.

30 How did Jake feel during a recent air display?

A relieved that plans for the day were successful

B concerned about the number of people watching

C impressed by the impact it had on the airport

SPEAKING (14 minutes)

You take the Speaking test with another candidate (possibly two candidates), referred to here as your partner. There are two examiners. One will speak to you and your partner and the other will be listening. Both examiners will award marks.

Part 1 (2 minutes (3 minutes for groups of three))

The examiner asks you and your partner questions about yourselves. You may be asked about things like 'your home town', 'your interests', 'your career plans', etc.

Part 2 (4 minutes (6 minutes for groups of three))

The examiner gives you two photographs and asks you to talk about them for one minute. The examiner then asks your partner a question about your photographs and your partner responds briefly.

Then the examiner gives your partner two different photographs. Your partner talks about these photographs for one minute. This time the examiner asks you a question about your partner's photographs and you respond briefly.

Part 3 (4 minutes (5 minutes for groups of three))

The examiner asks you and your partner to talk together. They give you a task to look at so you can think about and discuss an idea, giving reasons for your opinion. For example, you may be asked to think about some changes in the world, or about spending free time with your family. After you have discussed the task for about two minutes with your partner, the examiner will ask you a follow-up question, which you should discuss for a further minute.

Part 4 (4 minutes (6 minutes for groups of three))

The examiner asks some further questions, which leads to a more general discussion of what you have talked about in Part 3. You may comment on your partner's answers if you wish.

Test 2

READING AND USE OF ENGLISH (1 hour 15 minutes)

Part 1

For questions **1–8**, read the text below and decide which answer (**A**, **B**, **C** or **D**) best fits each gap. There is an example at the beginning (**0**).

Mark your answers **on the separate answer sheet.**

Example:

0 **A** gone along **B** come up **C** thought out **D** looked into

0	A	B	C	D
	▭	▬	▭	▭

Magic paper?

Scientists have **(0)** .... with a new type of paper that can be printed on and then used again up to 20 times. Users will be able to either remove the writing from the paper themselves, or **(1)** .... it to disappear over a period of time, after which the paper will be completely blank and ready to be printed on again. There is no significant change in quality between the first and the twentieth printout. Under normal **(2)** .... it seems that the writing will remain perfectly **(3)** .... for at least three days, long enough for most **(4)** .... purposes.

This new process does not **(5)** .... ink. Instead, the paper is printed on using a combination of chemicals and light. If users want the print to disappear more quickly, they can apply heat to the paper. This can take as little as ten minutes. The **(6)** .... is that in the future this paper will be **(7)** .... used, providing an environmentally friendly **(8)** .... to ordinary paper.

1	**A**	make	**B**	cause	**C**	expect	**D**	leave
2	**A**	situations	**B**	circumstances	**C**	contexts	**D**	settings
3	**A**	clear	**B**	obvious	**C**	evident	**D**	apparent
4	**A**	objective	**B**	practical	**C**	functional	**D**	constructive
5	**A**	insist	**B**	request	**C**	oblige	**D**	require
6	**A**	cause	**B**	wish	**C**	hope	**D**	reason
7	**A**	widely	**B**	broadly	**C**	largely	**D**	mainly
8	**A**	substitute	**B**	option	**C**	replacement	**D**	alternative

Part 2

For questions **9–16**, read the text below and think of the word which best fits each gap. Use only **one** word in each gap. There is an example at the beginning **(0)**.

Write your answers **IN CAPITAL LETTERS on the separate answer sheet.**

Example: | 0 | ONE |

The Freedom Ship

Imagine the largest ship you've ever seen, then try to imagine **(0)** .... far bigger. In fact, try to imagine a ship **(9)** .... size of a small island and big **(10)** .... to provide a permanent home for around 40,000 residents. Imagine this ship circling the globe once every two years, spending 70% of the time close to major cities and the rest following the warm weather as **(11)** .... sails between countries.

This was the aim of the designers of the Freedom Ship, **(12)** .... dream it was to create a vast floating city, complete **(13)** .... hospitals, schools, shops and even an airport. First proposed in 1994, it has been advertised as a new way of living, a unique lifestyle in a global community **(14)** .... suit all budgets. However, such an elaborate plan comes at an extremely high price. **(15)** .... a result, the designers have been unable to **(16)** .... their exciting ideas into practice. But who can tell what possibilities the future holds?

Part 3

For questions **17–24**, read the text below. Use the word given in capitals at the end of some of the lines to form a word that fits in the gap **in the same line**. There is an example at the beginning (**0**).

Write your answers **IN CAPITAL LETTERS on the separate answer sheet.**

Example: | 0 | A | W | A | R | E | N | E | S | S |

New Yorkers jump on giant bed

In New York, a man decided to make a video to raise **(0)** .... for	**AWARE**
a children's charity. His **(17)** .... was also to spread joy in a city	**INTEND**
which sometimes has a reputation for being cold and **(18)** .... So	**WELCOME**
he transported a giant bed around town and encouraged his fellow	
(19) .... to jump on it, then watched with	**CITY**
(20) .... as large numbers of people did so. Those who were more	**SATISFY**
(21) .... started to see which of their friends could jump the highest	**COMPETE**
in preference to just jumping up and down.	
His first thought had been just to use a mattress, but then a friend built a	
proper frame with the **(22)** .... to support six adults jumping around	**STRONG**
at the same time. He was afraid of getting a negative **(23)** .... from	**RESPOND**
some people who would think the idea was silly and **(24)** .... and	**CHILD**
refuse to do it. Most people who tried it, however, said the experience	
was really enjoyable and that they'd happily do it again!	

Part 4

For questions **25–30**, complete the second sentence so that it has a similar meaning to the first sentence, using the word given. **Do not change the word given**. You must use between **two** and **five** words, including the word given. Here is an example (**0**).

Example:

0 Prizes are given out when the school year finishes.

PLACE

Prize-giving .... end of the school year.

The gap can be filled by the words 'takes place at the', so you write:

Example:	**0**	*TAKES PLACE AT THE*

Write **only** the missing words **IN CAPITAL LETTERS on the separate answer sheet.**

---

25 I think I can come to your party after all.

SHOULD

I .... to your party after all.

26 Last year, the number of complaints about the leisure centre rose.

INCREASE

Last year, there .... the number of complaints about the leisure centre.

27 Marta always starts to talk about something else when I try to discuss the history project with her.

SUBJECT

Marta changes .... time I try to discuss the history project with her.

28 There will be bikes available for you to use during the school trip.

DISPOSAL

There will be bikes .... during the school trip.

29 My geography teacher expects a lot from us, so I'm working hard on this project.

EXPECTATIONS

My geography teacher .... of us, so I'm working hard on this project.

30 Sorry, I completely forgot the time so I missed the bus.

REALISE

Sorry, I .... the time was so I missed the bus.

Part 5

You are going to read an article about an astronomy club in the USA. For questions **31–36**, choose the answer (**A**, **B**, **C** or **D**) which you think fits best according to the text.

Mark your answers **on the separate answer sheet.**

A special astronomy club

A group of US teenagers study the night sky.

The teenage members of the Earth to Sky Calculus Club live in and around Bishop, a mountain town in the USA surrounded almost entirely by wilderness, to the east of the Sierra Nevada mountain range. Over the last few years, this isolated group has launched over 50 balloons to the edge of space, around 35 km above the Earth's surface. It's a long-running science project but with a bit of a twist: it's part astronomy experiment, part backcountry adventure, which is possibly why teenagers get involved. I join them one weekend in late spring. They are about to release a high-altitude balloon, hoping to record shooting stars. These occur when a rock or piece of metal travelling through space enters the Earth's atmosphere, producing a trail of light.

As it gets dark, the teenagers secure a soft insulated $5 lunch box to the bottom of the balloon. Inside is a camera, an instrument to measure altitude and a thermometer to gauge the changes along the ascent. Two GPS trackers are mounted on the outside of the lunch box to help the group to find it later. A gas tank, donated by an enthusiast in a neighbouring state, is used to inflate the balloon, which slowly grows to the size of a small car. An older boy had made a seven-hour round trip
line 29 to get hold of it. 'I didn't really mind,' he says. Anyway, for kids in this club, that's a given.

Finally, it's time for lift-off. 'Five, four, three, two, one,' they chant, and the balloon begins its ascent. Some of them run and track its path with powerful flashlights for as long as they are able, illuminating the creamy orb in the moonless sky. There is quiet, and a palpable sense of collective wonder. Then the balloon disappears into the night.

When the launch is over, most of the students go home, but a few stay to watch the shooting stars. A boy climbs into a sleeping bag and promptly falls asleep. 'We're the only ones talking,' says one girl in hushed tones. 'I know,' whispers another. A meteor shoots across the middle of the sky.

As a balloon rises, the air pressure lessens and the balloon expands until it's almost the size of a house. Then it pops in a dramatic explosion. A parachute helps the equipment inside the lunch box land safely back on Earth. The students will find it the following day, using the GPS trackers as a guide. Getting it back isn't straightforward, but that's part of the appeal. There is little inhabited land around Bishop, so the lunch box almost always lands somewhere in the middle of nowhere. 'To me, recoveries are a huge part of the program,' said the group's leader, who notes they've lost only two lunch boxes in 53 launches. 'Part of the journey has been becoming more familiar with this landscape in a way you never normally would.'

On this occasion, the lunch box had landed 84 km west of Bishop, but to get to it, the recovery team would have to drive south of the Sierra and then back up the western side of the mountain range. Then they'd have to agree whether driving or walking would be preferable
– things could turn treacherous if the lunch *line 68*
box was on a high peak, or even worse, up a very tall tree. 'It's important to keep in mind that these students are native to the Eastern Sierra,' their leader says. 'What may seem wild and perilous to some, is simply a way of life to others.'

In the end, it took them 11 hours to find the lunch box. It was in a canyon, high on a flat rock, in the middle of a cascading waterfall. The camera hadn't recorded any shooting stars. Sure, it's a bit of a disappointment, but it's one more tale of adventure to share with anyone who asks.

31 What does the writer say about the club in the first paragraph?

A The combination of activities offered makes it unusual.
B Its members have joined because there's little else to do.
C The projects it organises are over-ambitious.
D Its aims remain rather unclear.

32 What does 'it' refer to in line 29?

A the lunch box
B the balloon
C the gas tank
D the car

33 How does the writer say the group feel when the balloon takes off?

A disappointed to lose sight of it
B amazed that it has risen so quickly
C hopeful that they will recover it
D moved by the experience of it

34 What view does the group's leader express in the fifth paragraph?

A The recovery operations can be inconvenient.
B Learning so much about the area has been a bonus.
C The long journeys they make are annoying but necessary.
D Losing some lunch boxes has been a price worth paying.

35 What does 'things could turn treacherous' mean in line 68?

A The teenagers could appear irresponsible.
B The situation could put people at risk.
C The outcome could be unpredictable.
D Their efforts could prove inadequate.

36 What point is made in the sixth paragraph?

A People should respect the lifestyles of the inhabitants of an area.
B People have to make difficult decisions at some stage in their lives.
C People adopt attitudes that are affected by the environment they grow up in.
D People should exercise more caution when in unfamiliar environments.

Part 6

You are going to read an article about some seals that are using technology to their advantage. Six sentences have been removed from the article. Choose from the sentences **A–G** the one which fits each gap (**37–42**). There is one extra sentence which you do not need to use.

Mark your answers **on the separate answer sheet.**

Clever seals

Scientists believe some seals have discovered a new way to hunt for fish.

Tiny electronic devices attached to wild animals have become an increasingly common way for scientists to study those that are difficult to locate and follow on a day-to-day basis. The devices, known as 'acoustic tags', send out signals in the form of sound waves that the human ear cannot hear. The animals to which they are attached cannot hear them either, so are not disturbed by them. However, now it seems that clever seals are using them to their advantage to catch fish!

This finding was revealed in a recent study published by a team of researchers from the University of St. Andrews in Scotland. **37** ______ Previous research by another team had also indicated that while the sounds produced by acoustic tags could not be heard by the fish they were attached to, other animals that hunted the fish, like seals and sea lions, were able to detect the signal quite easily.

To verify if that was true, the St. Andrews University researchers selected a group of ten young grey seals that had been born in captivity and never lived in the wild. This meant that the marine animals had never encountered the ocean. **38** ______ The researchers placed the seals one at a time inside a pool that contained 20 boxes, only two of which contained fish – one with tags and the other without.

Each seal was allowed to enter the pool on a number of occasions to explore the boxes. In order to ensure that the seals were not depending on their memory, the fish were randomly moved to different boxes each time. There was initially no difference in the amount of time it took the seals to discover the tagged and untagged fish. **39** ______

What was even more interesting was that the more 'experienced' the seals became, the more frequently they visited the box containing the tagged fish. **40** ______

To confirm that the animals were in fact making use of the tags, the researchers conducted a second experiment using two boxes – one containing pieces of fish and the other just acoustic tags. **41** ______

While this experiment involved only seals, the researchers believe that other marine mammals may also be using the information to avoid predators. They are worried that sharks, for example, which have been tagged by scientists may be negatively affected, as the signals emitted by the acoustic tags could warn smaller animals of their presence and so prevent the sharks from catching their prey. Apart from messing up nature's food chain, another potential concern relating to the use of acoustic tags has arisen. **42** ______ Now that the secret is out, scientists will have to come up with another innovative way to conduct their studies – one that cannot be detected by clever marine animals.

A Nor had they been exposed to any kind of acoustic tag.

B It is that the conclusions reached by previous fish studies may not be reliable.

C This suggested that the seals had indeed figured out how to use the acoustic signals to their advantage.

D Nevertheless, this behaviour led the team to doubt whether their theory was correct.

E They had become interested in the idea that the tags might be having unexpected effects.

F Sure enough, the seals all went to the one that was sending out signals.

G However, after they had been in the pool a few times, they started locating the tagged fish much faster.

Part 7

You are going to read an article in which young people talk about their early experiences of going to football matches. For questions **43–52**, choose from the people (**A–D**). The people may be chosen more than once.

Mark your answers **on the separate answer sheet**.

Which person

says that one player was initially unsure of his success?	**43**	
says that they missed a big event in their team's history?	**44**	
was given a special treat to mark an amazing achievement?	**45**	
felt being a spectator gave them a sense of belonging?	**46**	
expresses admiration for a footballer on the other side?	**47**	
says they went to football matches on a regular basis?	**48**	
mentions that a member of their team showed great confidence regarding a match result?	**49**	
enjoyed an event they saw during the match more than the final outcome?	**50**	
has a lasting memory of viewing the pitch from high up?	**51**	
witnessed one of the early matches played by a very promising team member?	**52**	

Football matches

A Phoebe

It would have been impossible for a 10-year-old taken to the football stadium every other weekend, as I was, not to get sucked in by the atmosphere in the stands and out on the pitch. And to stand among the crowd of spectators was like being welcomed into one great big family. There was a heightened sense of glamour, too, as we had a player in our team who'd also played internationally. To me, he seemed to have been sent from another universe. Anyway, at least I got to witness some of the club's glory years, even though my first match was a whole two seasons after they'd won a major cup. Still, plenty of great memories – luckily, because the club hasn't done so well in recent years.

B Mark

I've been going to football matches ever since I was about six. When I think back, I can't remember the player's names so well, but I do remember that our best goal scorer, when I first started going, was a tall agile guy who'd just curl the ball into the back of the net. On one occasion he slammed it into the goal from 40 metres away before the goalkeeper even had time to raise his hands. I've never seen a better goal since, although I only got a really good view of it because my dad led us up the wrong steps in the stand, after the half-time break. It was followed by the best celebration: a fantastic pointing-at-the-skies moment. We won 2-1 but, to be honest, after that amazing spectacle, nothing else really mattered. Dad bought me a celebratory burger on the way home.

C Thomas

The first time I went to a football match was quite an experience. The club I supported had just knocked out the favourites from a national tournament, and every time I turned on the radio I heard our captain telling the press that the cup was as good as ours. There were 40,000 people packed into the stadium, but it was seeing the floodlit grounds below from the top of the steeply arranged seats that stuck in my mind. That was the moment I really fell in love with football. And then they kicked off. My team lost – a word combination I quickly got used to. That time it was due to one brilliant player scoring from 25 metres. Then his second goal went in and the final score was 2-1 to them. It was still amazing as far as I was concerned.

D Teresa

On my first ever visit to the stadium, my team were playing on a muddy pitch that got worse as the rain kept falling. But that didn't put one player off – a teenager who'd recently come up from the youth team and later went on to achieve great fame. He scored our only goal in the final minutes. I vaguely recall the ball bouncing over the goalkeeper, who'd come out to the edge of his area. He ran back and dived for it but slipped in the mud and couldn't keep it out of the net. The weather was so bad, the teenager could barely see what had happened and didn't realise at first that he'd actually scored. So there we go – pouring rain, muddy pitch, 5-1 defeat for my team, got soaked. And I still decided to support them!

WRITING (1 hour 20 minutes)

Part 1

You **must** answer this question. Write your answer in **140–190** words in an appropriate style **on the separate answer sheet**.

---

1 In your English class you have been talking about rules at home. Now your English teacher has asked you to write an essay for homework.

Write your essay using **all** the notes and giving reasons for your point of view.

'It's very important for young people to have rules at home.'

Do you agree?

Notes

Write about:

1. jobs around the house
2. behaviour during meal-times
3. .... (your own idea)

Part 2

Write an answer to **one** of the questions **2–4** in this part. Write your answer in **140–190** words in an appropriate style **on the separate answer sheet**. Put the question number in the box at the top of the answer sheet.

---

2 You have received this email from your English friend, Sam:

> Hi
>
> A friend of mine never seems to want to do the same things as I do, and I always end up doing things I'm not that interested in. I'm not sure what I should do about this as we actually get on really well with each other.
>
> Can you give me some advice?
>
> Thanks
>
> Sam

Write your **email**.

3 You recently saw this notice in an international magazine for teenagers:

> *Reviews wanted*
>
> **Family holidays**
>
> Do you know a good place to have a family holiday? If so, write us a review describing the place, explaining the benefits for different members of a family and saying why you especially recommend it.
>
> The best reviews will be published next month.

Write your **review**.

4 You have seen this announcement in an international magazine for schools:

> **Stories wanted**
>
> We are looking for stories for our new English-language magazine for teenagers. Your story must **begin** with this sentence:
>
> *Mark was walking along the beach one Saturday morning.*
>
> Your story must include:
> - a sound
> - a rescue

Write your **story**.

LISTENING (approximately 40 minutes)

Part 1

You will hear people talking in eight different situations.

For questions **1–8**, choose the best answer (**A**, **B** or **C**).

---

1 You hear two friends talking about a lesson on the subject of newspapers.

What do they agree about it?

A Some unusual ideas were expressed.

B A wide range of issues were covered.

C It was well-planned.

2 You hear a man talking about skateboarders in the past.

What is he doing?

A explaining the reputation they once had

B describing how attitudes towards them have changed

C suggesting reasons for their interest in the sport

3 You hear a girl talking about a diary she keeps.

Her main aim is to explain

A her reason for starting to write a diary.

B the effect that keeping a diary has on her.

C the different functions a diary can have.

4 You hear a boy talking about a weekly video he posts online in which he expresses his opinions.

What does he find most challenging?

A responding to criticism from other people

B producing original ideas on a regular basis

C coping with the amount of interest he gets

5 You hear part of a programme about sea creatures called sea dragons.

What does the man say about the different types of sea dragon?

A Their sources of food are becoming scarcer.

B They have names which reflect their appearance.

C Certain differences between them have only recently been discovered.

6 You hear two friends talking about a film they've seen.

What does the girl think about it?

A The storyline was too complicated to follow.

B The music was unsuitable for the subject matter.

C The main actor failed to live up to her expectations.

7 You hear a news item about a small town in Alaska called Whittier.

What is unusual about the town?

A Children can get to school without going outdoors.

B There is only one shop for the people to use.

C All residents live and work in one tall apartment block.

8 You hear two friends talking about a dance competition.

What do they agree about it?

A It should be held on another day.

B It will be more fun to watch than take part in.

C It's bound to be a great success.

Part 2

You will hear an astronomer called Steve Mitchell talking about his work. For questions **9–18**, complete the sentences with a word or short phrase.

Working as an astronomer

Steve first became interested in astronomy after watching a **(9)** .... on TV.

Steve says that as a teenager he particularly appreciated the **(10)** .... of the night sky.

Steve describes how excited he felt when he saw a **(11)** .... through his telescope.

Steve finds it surprising that the **(12)** .... in the universe are so varied.

Steve's ambition is to go on a trip to **(13)** .... one day.

Steve says that **(14)** .... can cause unexpected problems for inexperienced astronomers living in built-up areas.

Steve thinks finding a **(15)** .... is the best thing that beginners interested in astronomy could do.

Steve thinks the many **(16)** .... surrounding one planet would be easy for young astronomers to identify.

Steve says that amateur astronomers' important **(17)** .... include finding new stars.

Steve explains that **(18)** .... is the most important quality astronomers need to have.

Part 3

You will hear five short extracts in which teenagers are talking about a favourite book. For questions **19–23**, choose from the list (**A–H**) what each speaker says about the book. Use the letters only once. There are three extra letters which you do not need to use.

A I was drawn into it from the beginning.

B It's more humorous than other books by the same author.

C One of the characters reminds me of someone I know well.

D It used to belong to a relative of mine.

E It's set in a place I've visited.

F I was inspired to read it by a TV programme.

G It helped me to deal with a situation in my own life.

H There are interesting descriptions of people in it.

Speaker 1		**19**
Speaker 2		**20**
Speaker 3		**21**
Speaker 4		**22**
Speaker 5		**23**

Part 4

You will hear an interview with a man called Josh Reed, who teaches people how to climb trees. For questions **24–30**, choose the best answer (**A**, **B** or **C**).

---

24 When Josh tells people what he does, they are usually

A confused about what his job involves.

B surprised that there is such a job.

C critical of his choice of job.

25 What appealed to Josh as a child about climbing trees?

A the excitement of doing something his parents disapproved of

B the chance to face up to a physical challenge

C the contrast with his other daily activities

26 What does Josh think now about the job he had looking after trees in public places?

A He continued doing it for too long.

B It was the obvious work for him to go into.

C The training he received for it was limited.

27 Josh says his main aim in offering his tree-climbing courses was to

A make people more knowledgeable about trees.

B show people the health benefits of this activity.

C change people's attitude to the environment.

28 Why is Josh against climbing very tall trees?

A It's dangerous for ordinary people to try it.

B It's unfair to disturb the wildlife in them.

C It's wrong to run the risk of damaging them.

29 What impressed Josh about the group he recently taught?

A how effectively they dealt with a problem

B how carefully they listened to his advice

C how quickly they learnt climbing skills

30 What does Josh look forward to doing in the future?

A developing new tree-climbing techniques

B having the chance to climb trees in different parts of the world

C spending more time promoting tree climbing as a leisure activity

SPEAKING (14 minutes)

You take the Speaking test with another candidate (possibly two candidates), referred to here as your partner. There are two examiners. One will speak to you and your partner and the other will be listening. Both examiners will award marks.

Part 1 (2 minutes (3 minutes for groups of three))

The examiner asks you and your partner questions about yourselves. You may be asked about things like 'your home town', 'your interests', 'your career plans', etc.

Part 2 (4 minutes (6 minutes for groups of three))

The examiner gives you two photographs and asks you to talk about them for one minute. The examiner then asks your partner a question about your photographs and your partner responds briefly.

Then the examiner gives your partner two different photographs. Your partner talks about these photographs for one minute. This time the examiner asks you a question about your partner's photographs and you respond briefly.

Part 3 (4 minutes (5 minutes for groups of three))

The examiner asks you and your partner to talk together. They give you a task to look at so you can think about and discuss an idea, giving reasons for your opinion. For example, you may be asked to think about some changes in the world, or about spending free time with your family. After you have discussed the task for about two minutes with your partner, the examiner will ask you a follow-up question, which you should discuss for a further minute.

Part 4 (4 minutes (6 minutes for groups of three))

The examiner asks some further questions, which leads to a more general discussion of what you have talked about in Part 3. You may comment on your partner's answers if you wish.

Test 3

READING AND USE OF ENGLISH (1 hour 15 minutes)

Part 1

For questions **1–8**, read the text below and decide which answer (**A**, **B**, **C** or **D**) best fits each gap. There is an example at the beginning (**0**).

Mark your answers **on the separate answer sheet.**

Example:

0 **A** far **B** alike **C** even **D** again

0	A	B	C	D
	▭	▭	▬	▭

Clever crows

Did you know that crows are really intelligent birds, maybe **(0)** .... as intelligent as young children? Scientists have **(1)** .... at this conclusion following a series of experiments **(2)** .... in the UK and New Zealand. In one, a crow worked out how to use tools to **(3)** .... an eight-stage puzzle and find food that had been placed out of **(4)** .... The crow had never seen the complex puzzle before but managed to solve it in a **(5)** .... short time, which is something many young children would **(6)** .... to do. In another experiment, six crows had to carry **(7)** .... various tasks. In one task, the birds had to learn that if they dropped heavy objects into tubes filled with water, the water level would rise, **(8)** .... them to catch food rewards floating on the surface. The crows soon understood that the most effective way of doing this was to choose tubes with high water levels and to select objects that would sink.

1	**A**	approached	**B**	come	**C**	got	**D**	arrived
2	**A**	adopted	**B**	conducted	**C**	operated	**D**	established
3	**A**	conclude	**B**	decide	**C**	complete	**D**	secure
4	**A**	reach	**B**	access	**C**	way	**D**	limit
5	**A**	commonly	**B**	relatively	**C**	generally	**D**	routinely
6	**A**	compete	**B**	fight	**C**	struggle	**D**	challenge
7	**A**	on	**B**	through	**C**	off	**D**	out
8	**A**	enabling	**B**	letting	**C**	ensuring	**D**	confirming

Part 2

For questions **9–16**, read the text below and think of the word which best fits each gap. Use only **one** word in each gap. There is an example at the beginning (**0**).

Write your answers **IN CAPITAL LETTERS on the separate answer sheet.**

Example: | **0** | T O |

Young snowboarder

Meet Jack Preston, the latest – and youngest – star on the snowboarding scene. He's won competitions, regularly competes against adults and hopes **(0)** .... compete in the next Winter Olympics, but he's only 12 years old. According to his trainer, there are professional snowboarders who may never achieve **(9)** .... he has, and it is no exaggeration to say he's the best young snowboarder in the country. Jack's inspired by his parents, keen snowboarders themselves, **(10)** .... first introduced him to snowboarding **(11)** .... a very young age. Jack took to the sport naturally and was soon racing down the slopes. **(12)** .... then, his snowboarding has gone from strength to strength and he now **(13)** .... much of his free time practising and travelling around the world to **(14)** .... part in competitions. His parents make sure this doesn't interfere **(15)** .... his school life and Jack says he's grateful for the opportunity to **(16)** .... so many great experiences. Keep an eye out for Jack Preston at the next Winter Olympics!

Part 3

For questions **17–24**, read the text below. Use the word given in capitals at the end of some of the lines to form a word that fits in the gap **in the same line**. There is an example at the beginning (**0**).

Write your answers **IN CAPITAL LETTERS on the separate answer sheet.**

Example:	**0**	N	A	T	U	R	A	L

Oregon's Lost Lake

In Oregon in the US there's a **(0)** .... wonder called Lost Lake.	**NATURE**
During winter, it looks like any other large lake. However, in late	
spring the water **(17)** .... , transforming the 'lake' into a beautiful	**APPEAR**
field of grass. This may seem **(18)** .... , but in fact there's a logical	**MYSTERY**
(19) .... : the lake lies on an ancient volcano, and there is a	**EXPLAIN**
continuous flow of water through a tunnel in the lake bed created	
by lava, the hot, liquid rock that came out of the volcano when it	
was **(20)**	**ACT**
The lake fills up **(21)** .... during the rainy season in autumn.	**STEADY**
Because the lava tunnel measures less than two metres in diameter, the	
water is **(22)** .... to escape quickly, so there's more water coming	**ABLE**
into the lake than leaving it. That's why the lake fills up, reaching a	
maximum **(23)** .... of fifty metres. It remains full as snow from	**DEEP**
the **(24)** .... mountains melts. But once the snow has disappeared,	**SURROUND**
the gradual loss of water causes the lake to vanish.	

Part 4

For questions **25–30**, complete the second sentence so that it has a similar meaning to the first sentence, using the word given. **Do not change the word given**. You must use between **two** and **five** words, including the word given. Here is an example (**0**).

Example:

0 Prizes are given out when the school year finishes.

PLACE

Prize-giving .... end of the school year.

The gap can be filled by the words 'takes place at the', so you write:

Example:	**0**	*TAKES PLACE AT THE*

Write only the missing words **IN CAPITAL LETTERS on the separate answer sheet.**

---

25 Don't ask Jim to join the football team – he really doesn't want to.

USE

It's .... Jim to join the football team – he really doesn't want to.

26 It's a pity I forgot to bring my coat with me, because it's absolutely freezing!

WISH

I .... to bring my coat with me, because it's absolutely freezing!

27 'You really shouldn't have upset your sister!' Dad said to me.

OFF

Dad told .... upsetting my sister.

28 Unfortunately, I don't know much about the history of the castles in the area.

UNFAMILIAR

Unfortunately, ... the history of the castles in this area.

29 They didn't expect many people would come to the beach party because of the weather.

EXPECTED

Few people .... up at the beach party because of the weather.

30 It's a pity Sarah didn't tell us which bus to take to her house.

OUGHT

Sarah .... us which bus to take to her house.

Part 5

You are going to read an extract from an interview with a palaeontologist, a scientist who studies dinosaurs and other creatures that lived millions of years ago. For questions **31–36**, choose the answer (**A**, **B**, **C** or **D**) which you think fits best according to the text.

Mark your answers **on the separate answer sheet**.

Walking with Dinosaurs

Chloe Morgan readily admits science, let alone Palaeontology, hadn't held too much appeal for her, at least not until she was fifteen. Even then, it happened more by accident than design. 'My younger brother was going through the dinosaur phase that's so common among children, and which I hadn't experienced. In fact, I tended to dismiss it. I reluctantly lent him a hand with a science project, and when I came across an article about some of the recent discoveries in the field, it just blew my mind. I knew immediately that this was something I wanted to commit myself to.'

I am curious to know what encouragement she got because Palaeontology was by no means a common career choice for young people at that time. 'I remember meeting my first professional palaeontologist,' she laughs. 'This guy, Matt Cornelius, was famous already, despite being quite young. At first I was a nervous wreck, even though he had a reputation for being approachable and easy-going. I was still worried he'd think I was just an annoying kid pestering him with my questions. But I felt more at ease when he showed so much patience and willingness to listen.'

I cannot resist bringing up the question of the portrayal of palaeontologists in movies and TV shows. Chloe frowns for a moment. 'I have to admit that films such as *Jurassic Park* featuring dinosaurs created by special effects technology have led to a huge surge in public interest in these creatures, though not necessarily in Palaeontology more generally. However much I welcome this, I think the relatively few examples of palaeontologists depicted in the cinema are misleading. What irritates me is that we're either stereotyped as eccentric geniuses or rather geeky losers, figures of fun who don't know how to relate to people. And films fail to represent accurately the everyday reality of our working lives.' I ask her to explain.

'My job is remarkably varied. I spend lots of time digging up dinosaur bones, but I also have to put in long hours in laboratories, analysing fossils, and writing for scientific publications.'

While it's not necessarily something Chloe is required to do on a daily basis, there's also the question of communicating scientific findings to the public, if time allows. The role of explaining and clarifying is one she takes seriously. 'There are a lot of misunderstandings and misconceptions about science, and though I know colleagues who are reluctant to take on such a challenge and don't want to be distracted from doing research, I see dealing with these issues as something I ought to do. I like to reach out to young people in particular, because it's important to let them know about all aspects of science. Talking about dinosaurs is one way to get children fired up about the natural world, and widen their horizons. They can start to appreciate other branches of science and to grasp more complex scientific ideas.'

The recent TV documentary *Walking with Dinosaurs* was a great opportunity for Chloe to influence the way dinosaurs are portrayed on screen, as she was invited to offer her advice. 'I had a fairly easy time of it because there was very little that I needed to comment on; it was mostly checking that the dinosaurs shown did exist together in the same time period. We succeeded in attracting audiences of all ages because we've learnt such a tremendous amount about dinosaurs recently.' This means that the dinosaurs in the documentary are easily the most life-like that have ever been portrayed.

Why does Chloe feel dinosaurs continue to fascinate us and remain the focus of ongoing research? 'I suspect that they speak to the innate explorer in all of us. Our imaginations are drawn to the unfamiliar and the prospect of discovery. And at a time when our world seems to be shrinking, prehistoric creatures remind us that there is still more out there to be discovered. And Palaeontology is a great form of time travel.'

31 Chloe says she became seriously interested in Palaeontology because

A she was astonished by something she read by chance.
B she had always been enthusiastic about related subjects.
C she was keen to share her brother's passion for the subject.
D she was aware that others seemed to know a great deal about it.

32 What does 'this' refer to in line 37?

A the number of films about dinosaurs
B the new desire for information about dinosaurs
C the greater public understanding of Palaeontology
D the special effects technology used by film makers

33 What does Chloe feel about the way palaeontologists are shown in films and on TV?

A disappointed that a false impression is given of them
B pleased because there is a range of different personalities
C resigned to putting up with the unfair criticism they receive
D amused by some of the situations they find themselves in

34 What does Chloe say about communicating with the public about Palaeontology?

A She is delighted she can devote so much time to it.
B She worries that it may prevent her from focusing on research.
C She is critical of some scientists' lack of ability to do it well.
D She feels it is her duty to make science more comprehensible.

35 What does the expression 'widen their horizons' mean in line 66?

A make them more tolerant of different things
B change their view of what's important in life
C make them aware of new ideas
D encourage them to travel more

36 Chloe thinks that dinosaurs continue to appeal to us because

A they make us appreciate that the world remains a mysterious place.
B they are creatures that it is hard to believe ever existed.
C they require interesting research in order for us to understand them.
D they provide an escape from the boredom of our everyday lives.

Part 6

You are going to read an article about the discovery of a new basic taste. Six sentences have been removed from the article. Choose from the sentences **A–G** the one which fits each gap (**37–42**). There is one extra sentence which you do not need to use.

Mark your answers **on the separate answer sheet.**

A new taste

Scientists believe they have found a new basic taste – beyond sour, sweet, salty, bitter and umami.

For hundreds of years, scientists have known about four basic, or 'primary' tastes: sour, sweet, salty and bitter. More recently, a Japanese chemist discovered a fifth primary taste, a savoury taste called umami. And now, researchers believe they have even found a sixth primary taste, and this may well affect the way in which we think about our food.

We experience the five distinct tastes because they react with our taste buds, the sensory organs in our mouths that allow us to distinguish between different tastes. There are thousands of these taste buds on the human tongue and all around the inside of our mouths. So, how we experience a mouthful of food really does depend on how the chemicals in the food affect our taste buds. Scientists now believe that fat may affect our taste buds in a similar way to other tastes, such as sour and sweet. We've known for some time that taste buds recognise fat. Scientists have, therefore, speculated that fat may produce a taste of its own which is distinguishable from the five other primary tastes. **37** ______

The researchers conducted two experiments. **38** ______ In the first, participants were given liquids that had one of six different tastes: sweet, salty, sour, bitter, umami and fatty. They were then asked to sort them into groups, as they believed were necessary. The participants had little trouble identifying sweet, salty and sour as unique tastes, but, interestingly, they put the remaining three all together into a single, separate group.

The researchers then took things a stage further. **39** ______ In the next experiment, they only gave participants solutions containing the three remaining tastes, and this time the participants had no difficulty separating them into three distinct groups. 'It was really very telling,' said Mattes, one of the scientists. 'We already knew that people have a taste receptor for fatty acids; now we know that it's a distinguishable taste.'

Fat, as everyone experiences it, is made up of three fatty acids. The combination of the three gives fat the creaminess we associate with it. The kind of fat Mattes is talking about is actually only in one of those three fatty acids. It's the one that gives us the taste that is unique to fat. A primary taste can only be called that if it shares no characteristics with the other primary tastes. The fact that people can so easily recognise fat as a different kind of taste is evidence that it is another primary taste. When you eat a food that contains fat, you don't immediately perceive the taste produced by this particular fatty acid. **40** ______

As a taste on its own, fat is pretty unappealing. 'It's very harsh,' said Mattes. 'It doesn't taste good.' But then, neither do some of the other primary tastes, such as bitter or sour. However, when added to other ingredients, it contributes greatly to the appeal of food, as is the case when it is used in combination with cocoa beans to make chocolate, for example. Many things are unpleasant in isolation, in fact. **41** ______

The impact of Mattes' research could extend well beyond the reach of his lab, to what appears on our plates. **42** ______ 'Understanding this could have huge implications for the food industry,' he said. If food manufacturers begin to concentrate on the flavour of fat as well as the creamy texture of it in our mouths, our food might actually start to taste better.'

A Fat is a perfect example of this.

B There isn't a firm agreement about what characteristics are necessary.

C That's when a clear division surfaced.

D Now there's evidence that it does.

E But it's there, and it's distinct.

F And, more specifically, it may affect how it tastes.

G This was to find out whether fat could be another of the basic tastes.

Part 7

You are going to read an article in which four students talk about subjects they enjoyed studying at school. For questions **43–52**, choose from the people (**A–D**). The people may be chosen more than once.

Mark your answers **on the separate answer sheet**.

Which girl

was shown the appeal of a subject she hadn't previously considered?	**43**	
says that she has learnt to solve complicated problems effectively?	**44**	
appreciates that a subject is of interest to diverse groups of people?	**45**	
sometimes received negative comments about her work?	**46**	
hid her true feelings about what her future might hold?	**47**	
felt that she had little chance of achieving an ambition?	**48**	
was frustrated at a lack of opportunity to be creative?	**49**	
enjoyed observing practical demonstrations in the subject?	**50**	
can understand why she was discouraged from studying something?	**51**	
found that potentially dull material was brought to life?	**52**	

Favourite subjects

A Tamsin

My Latin and Greek teacher taught me an invaluable lesson – that if you can excel at only one thing, then exploit that fully. I was a bit bored at school, and although I pretended otherwise, I was actually rather concerned about what lay ahead when I eventually left. But for some reason I'd always had an interest in the wonders of classical civilisation. The teacher loved her subject, and though she didn't hold back on the criticism when I messed up, she praised me to the skies when I met her expectations. She made what could simply have been dusty, dry books relevant to the modern world. I became fascinated not only with understanding the way society works, but also what makes people tick and how they deal with problems in life – and that's exactly what the ancient Greek tragedies are all about. And now I'm studying all this at university, and I feel really mentally stimulated.

B Bella

I liked art at school and, at one point, I even thought about studying it at university. But my parents put an end to that idea, as they said the subject wasn't appropriate for someone with my academic ability. Looking back I can see their point, but I felt I really needed some sort of outlet for my artistic ideas. Then, I discovered poetry, thanks to an outstanding teacher, who opened my eyes to the power of words, and encouraged me to go on to study English literature at university, which I'm now doing. And recently, I've taken to visiting museums, at quiet times, when the lack of bustling crowds means that you can stare at a painting or sculpture for as long as you want. Those visits are really important to me, and on my course I find I'm benefitting from the extra dimension that art brings to my reasoning.

C Karina

When I was at school, I always wanted to become a writer of some kind, although it somehow just felt hopelessly unrealistic. But I read an enormous amount, and loved playing around with words, so English literature was at the top of my list of favourite subjects. And studying it has given me more than I could ever have imagined. I've come to understand that modern works can be read for their underlying meaning rather than just the simple beauty of their prose. Now I've grasped that, the subject has become transformed for me into something with even greater significance. I realise that literature connects with people's lives and speaks to people no matter what their background might be. And, for me, the thrill of uncovering the hidden messages contained in a work of literature hasn't diminished in any way.

D Holly

At school, I always found the laws of physics fascinating to study, and memorable to see in action in classroom experiments. Luckily I was really good at maths, so the calculations we had to do weren't as taxing to me as they were to other students. And I got really carried away with experimenting – I made a device to measure magnetic fields with lasers. Physics is the study of the basic rules governing the universe, and the impact they have on our everyday lives. Studying it has helped me to develop a more analytical approach to any issue I have to deal with. It's given me the confidence to break down tricky tasks into manageable parts. And that has been really beneficial to me in my physics course at university.

WRITING (1 hour 20 minutes)

Part 1

You **must** answer this question. Write your answer in **140–190** words in an appropriate style **on the separate answer sheet**.

---

1 In your English class you have been talking about the opportunities teenagers have. Now your English teacher has asked you to write an essay for homework.

Write your essay using **all** the notes and giving reasons for your point of view.

'Young people nowadays have many more opportunities than young people had in the past.' Do you agree?

Notes

Write about:

1. education
2. travel
3. .... (your own idea)

Part 2

Write an answer to one of the questions **2–4** in this part. Write your answer in **140–190** words in an appropriate style **on the separate answer sheet**. Put the question number in the box at the top of the answer sheet.

---

2 You have seen this announcement in an English-language magazine for teenagers:

> *Stories wanted*
>
> We are looking for stories for our new English-language magazine for teenagers.
> Your story must **begin** with this sentence:
>
> *This was our first camping trip and we were really excited.*
>
> Your story must include:
>
> - a storm
> - a problem

Write your **story**.

3 You see this notice in an international magazine for teenagers:

> *Articles wanted*
>
> **School Rules!**
>
> Which rules at your school do you agree with and which ones do you think are unfair?
>
> Why is it important for students to have rules at school?
>
> The best articles will be published next month.

Write your **article**.

4 You recently saw this notice on a shopping website:

> *Reviews wanted*
>
> **Games and Toy Shops**
>
> Do you know a good shop which sells games or toys? If so, write us a review describing the shop and what it sells. Explain why the shop is a particularly good place to buy games or toys.
>
> The best reviews will be published next month.

Write your **review**.

LISTENING (approximately 40 minutes)

Part 1

You will hear people talking in eight different situations.

For questions **1–8**, choose the best answer (**A**, **B** or **C**).

---

1 You hear part of an interview with a tennis player after a match.

How does she feel?

A disappointed to have been injured

B grateful for the help she's received

C impressed by her opponent's performance

2 You hear two friends talking about a comedy show they went to see.

What do they agree about?

A how unsuitable the venue was

B how enthusiastic the audience was

C how original the comedian's humour was

3 You hear part of a radio phone-in programme about cycling in cities.

What is the caller doing?

A criticising the lack of cycling facilities

B encouraging people to take up cycling

C complaining about the way cyclists behave

4 You hear two friends discussing an article about junk food.

What does the girl suggest about it?

A It won't appeal to many people she knows.

B It contains information that is inaccurate.

C It is unlikely to affect the way she lives.

5 You hear a teacher talking about a large picture her students are painting to be displayed.

Why does the teacher want her students to paint the picture?

A to improve their ability to work as a team

B to make them aware of art in the area

C to encourage them to think creatively

6 You hear a boy telling a friend about a trip he went on with his father.

What does he say about it?

A He appreciated his father's attempts to please him.

B He was confident of his father's ability to organise things.

C He admired his father's knowledge of other places.

7 You hear a girl talking about a science experiment at her school.

She says that the experiment

A didn't work as well as intended.

B had an unexpected consequence.

C demonstrated an important scientific principle.

8 You hear two friends discussing an experiment into the effects of spending time in space.

What do they both think about it?

A They're interested to learn more.

B They admire the participants' courage.

C They'd be reluctant to do something similar.

Part 2

You will hear an interview with a boy called Luke Tyler, who took part in a desert marathon race. For questions **9–18**, complete the sentences with a word or short phrase.

Desert marathon race

The **(9)** .... for competitors are the same each year.

In his backpack, Luke made sure he put a **(10)** .... that didn't weigh very much.

When getting ready for the race, Luke thinks that his **(11)** .... helped him more than anything else.

Before the race, Luke was nervous about the danger of **(12)** .... in the desert.

Luke thinks he should have eaten more **(13)** .... during the marathon.

The runners stopped at places known as **(14)** .... where they could have a short rest.

Luke is pleased that he chose the right sort of **(15)** .... for the race.

Luke says the **(16)** .... were the most memorable things he saw in the desert.

Luke threw away some **(17)** .... which were items he didn't need.

Luke mentions that there were **(18)** .... which carried some larger items needed for overnight stops.

Part 3

You will hear five short extracts in which teenagers are talking about what's called a survival course, where they learnt the skills you need to live in a forest. For questions **19–23**, choose from the list (**A–H**) how each speaker felt during the course. Use the letters only once. There are three extra letters which you do not need to use.

A irritated by other students' behaviour

B concerned about the possibility of falling ill

C enthusiastic about working in a team

D frustrated by the time it took to do something

E impressed by someone's ability

F disappointed to miss out on something

G grateful for the opportunity to do something unusual

H surprised by how challenging some of the tasks were

Speaker	Answer	Question
Speaker 1		**19**
Speaker 2		**20**
Speaker 3		**21**
Speaker 4		**22**
Speaker 5		**23**

Part 4

You will hear an interview with a man called Danny Taylor, who is a record producer with his own recording studio. For questions **24–30**, choose the best answer (**A**, **B** or **C**).

---

24 Why did Danny decide to start his recording studio?

A He had difficulty finding a job in the music industry.

B He was keen to work with a variety of musicians.

C He wanted to record more of his own music.

25 When asked about the way his studio has developed, Danny says he's

A proud of the reputation he's built up.

B relieved that his business has kept going so long.

C frustrated about having to do certain kinds of work.

26 What does Danny say about the location of his studio?

A It differs from many other studios.

B It affects the style of music made there.

C It puts off younger bands and musicians.

27 What does Danny say about the behaviour of bands he works with?

A The way they interact is not reflected in their music.

B The stress involved in recording often leads to arguments.

C The image presented in the media is usually misleading.

28 What does Danny find hardest about his work?

A criticising musicians who lack talent

B deciding which bands he wants to work with

C dealing with the demands of well-known musicians

29 What does Danny think is his greatest strength as a music producer?

A his skill at helping inexperienced musicians improve

B his ability to make a song sound original

C his awareness of what will sell well

30 What advice does Danny offer people interested in becoming music producers?

A Remember that music production requires a great deal of commitment.

B Keep up-to-date with the latest music production technology.

C Find a course with links to the music industry.

SPEAKING (14 minutes)

You take the Speaking test with another candidate (possibly two candidates), referred to here as your partner. There are two examiners. One will speak to you and your partner and the other will be listening. Both examiners will award marks.

Part 1 (2 minutes (3 minutes for groups of three))

The examiner asks you and your partner questions about yourselves. You may be asked about things like 'your home town', 'your interests', 'your career plans', etc.

Part 2 (4 minutes (6 minutes for part three))

The examiner gives you two photographs and asks you to talk about them for one minute.
The examiner then asks your partner a question about your photographs and your partner responds briefly.

Then the examiner gives your partner two different photographs. Your partner talks about these photographs for one minute. This time the examiner asks you a question about your partner's photographs and you respond briefly.

Part 3 (4 minutes (5 minutes for groups of three))

The examiner asks you and your partner to talk together. They give you a task to look at so you can think about and discuss an idea, giving reasons for your opinion. For example, you may be asked to think about some changes in the world, or about spending free time with your family. After you have discussed the task for about two minutes with your partner, the examiner will ask you a follow-up question, which you should discuss for a further minute.

Part 4 (4 minutes (6 minutes for groups of three))

The examiner asks some further questions, which leads to a more general discussion of what you have talked about in Part 3. You may comment on your partner's answers if you wish.

Test 4

READING AND USE OF ENGLISH (1 hour 15 minutes)

Part 1

For questions **1–8**, read the text below and decide which answer (**A**, **B**, **C** or **D**) best fits each gap. There is an example at the beginning (**0**).

Mark your answers **on the separate answer sheet.**

Example:

0 **A** careless **B** casual **C** comfortable **D** chance

0	A	B	C	D
	▭	▬	▭	▭

Computer games may be good for the brain!

Playing computer games is no longer just a **(0)** .... pastime. Researchers are therefore increasingly curious to discover whether it **(1)** .... learning and, if so, how. A recent study has **(2)** .... that gamers are more efficient at visual task learning (learning by watching), than non-gamers.

In the study, keen gamers were compared with people who had rarely, if **(3)** .... , played video games. Each group was trained in two visual tasks. Improving visual learning takes time; usually, if a second task is **(4)** .... before the brain has had a chance to learn how to do the first one, it results in a decline in performance. So the following day, the participants were asked to **(5)** .... the same tasks again. The frequent gamers showed great **(6)** .... in both tasks, but the non-gamers' performance on the first task became worse. The scientists are not sure why this is the **(7)** .... but believe the learning process may be speeded up by the vast amount of visual training frequent gamers are **(8)** .... to over the years.

1	**A**	adapts	**B**	affects	**C**	relates	**D**	concerns
2	**A**	established	**B**	supposed	**C**	presented	**D**	examined
3	**A**	even	**B**	hardly	**C**	ever	**D**	yet
4	**A**	developed	**B**	inserted	**C**	raised	**D**	introduced
5	**A**	take up	**B**	carry out	**C**	get over	**D**	put forward
6	**A**	increase	**B**	advance	**C**	development	**D**	progress
7	**A**	case	**B**	fact	**C**	circumstance	**D**	position
8	**A**	supplied	**B**	provided	**C**	exposed	**D**	revealed

Part 2

For questions **9–16**, read the text below and think of the word which best fits each gap. Use only **one** word in each gap. There is an example at the beginning (**0**).

Write your answers **IN CAPITAL LETTERS on the separate answer sheet.**

Example: | **0** | *A* |

The Crystal Palace dinosaurs

The Crystal Palace dinosaurs are **(0)** .... collection of over 30 statues. They stand proudly overlooking a park in the London suburb of the same name. The park and dinosaur displays are open to the public and are free to visit. School groups frequently go and look at the dinosaurs, but **(9)** .... help preserve them, the statues are viewed from a distance and cannot **(10)** .... climbed. Created in around 1854, they were the first ever attempt anywhere in the world to represent dinosaurs as full-scale, three-dimensional, active creatures.

Some of the statues are dramatically different when **(11)** .... comes to comparing them with modern interpretations of dinosaurs. Which experts in the 1850s decided what the statues should look **(12)** .... is a subject of historical debate. However, research clearly shows that experts at the time **(13)** .... different interpretations of the dinosaurs, and these differences of opinion **(14)** .... reflected in the statues currently **(15)** .... display at Crystal Palace. The way in **(16)** .... these various interpretations have evolved demonstrates how scientific ideas often develop.

Part 3

For questions **17–24**, read the text below. Use the word given in capitals at the end of some of the lines to form a word that fits in the gap **in the same line**. There is an example at the beginning (**0**).

Write your answers **IN CAPITAL LETTERS on the separate answer sheet.**

Example: | **0** | T | H | O | U | G | H | T |

Food miles

Have you ever given any **(0)** .... to how far your food has	**THINK**
travelled before it arrives at your local shop? You might be	
surprised at the distance, or number of 'food miles' involved. And	
this isn't an easy **(17)** .... to make. However, some people are	**CALCULATE**
becoming **(18)** .... concerned that ignoring the issue of food	**INCREASE**
miles when shopping is **(19)** .... and can have a negative	**RESPONSIBLE**
impact on the environment. Buying food that has been **(20)**	**PRODUCT**
locally may appear to be the answer, but there are other factors	
to take into **(21)** .... For example, in the UK it may be more	**CONSIDER**
(22) .... friendly to import tomatoes rather than grow them, because	**ENVIRONMENT**
the **(23)** .... British weather can mean that a lot of electricity	**PREDICT**
is needed to heat greenhouses. It's difficult to know what the best	
solution is, but a good first step might be for **(24)** .... to do more of	**CONSUME**
their shopping in markets, where food tends to have less packaging.	

Part 4

For questions **25–30**, complete the second sentence so that it has a similar meaning to the first sentence, using the word given. **Do not change the word given**. You must use between **two** and **five** words, including the word given. Here is an example (**0**).

Example:

0 Prizes are given out when the school year finishes.

PLACE

Prize-giving .... end of the school year.

The gap can be filled by the words 'takes place at the', so you write:

Example:	**0**	*TAKES PLACE AT THE*

Write **only** the missing words **IN CAPITAL LETTERS on the separate answer sheet**.

---

25 It hasn't stopped raining all day so I can't go out!

WOULD

I .... raining so I could go out!

26 If chemistry is what you want to study next year, don't let your friends discourage you.

PUT

Don't let your friends .... studying chemistry next year, if that's what you want to do.

27 As far as I know, Mary's not back from holiday until next week.

BEST

To .... knowledge, Mary's not back from holiday until next week.

28 Membership fees for the after-school football club should be reduced significantly.

SIGNIFICANT

There needs .... in membership fees for the after-school football club.

29 The door was stuck and I couldn't open it, despite trying really hard.

MATTER

The door was stuck and I couldn't open it, ... tried.

30 How did Michael persuade you to help him with his project?

TALK

How did Michael .... him with his project?

Part 5

You are going to read an article about a teenager who is talking about long family car journeys. For questions **31–36**, choose the answer (**A**, **B**, **C** or **D**) which you think fits best according to the text.

Mark your answers **on the separate answer sheet**.

Family road trips

By Ben Robinson, aged 16

I'm just going to say this once, for the record: when you're travelling by car somewhere with your family, even when you're six years old, the chances are you know full well that you're not 'there yet,' even as you're asking over and over 'Are we there yet?' And anyway, the truth of the matter is, once you get there it's not 'there' anymore, is it? It's 'here'. So if you really think there's a chance that you're 'there' yet, you should be asking 'Are we *here* yet?' And I'm pretty sure there's no one who wishes they were 'there yet' more than the mums and dads fielding that question over and over every single long car trip.

I mean, seriously – what are us kids complaining about? Just think about it. Wouldn't you prefer to be lounging in the back seat, with nothing being demanded of you? So you watch endless DVDs that you've never seemed to get round to seeing before, listen to music, perhaps indulge in a few of the puzzles you've had for ages but not done, as the scenic vistas roll on by endlessly outside the window.

And acting as co-pilot in the passenger seat, map in hand, there'll be mum or dad, whose function is to dole out juice boxes, and cookies, or to adjust the radio station and temperature to whatever is requested – in short, to keep it all running smoothly and be the on-the-road concierge! Are we there yet? I hope not.

That is, of course, until someone in the car does something unthinkable – in my case generally my younger brother, Tim. Something like ... putting his foot on my side of the seat. What? He can't do that! So I put my foot on his side. And then it's his other foot, and then a hand, and next thing you know he's hurled his whole body over into my space and a fight has erupted. And the driver and co-pilot start reaching back and separating us as the car accelerates and swerves. They heatedly tell the younger sibling off, saying he should stay in his own seat and keep his hands to himself. This restores civility for a while. And the scenic wonders, steeped in history, continue rolling by.

And pretty soon after that, I'm trying to read, and suddenly I feel something – a draught blowing across my arm. But the car's not going that fast and the window's not even open. So where's it coming from? My vengeful sibling is in the next seat, discreetly but purposefully channeling his breath onto me. He's on his side, perfectly legitimately, not touching me – so he's got me on a technicality. Just breathing. What's the problem with that? The anger escalates. Tim gets yelled at, there's more swerving. Then slowly the madness subsides again – for now.

Over the years, Dad's developed strategies for dealing with us kids on the back seat. For example, his response to the question 'Are we there yet?' has frequently been, 'Yup. We're here. Get out of the car.'

'But Dad. We're still on the highway, going 70 miles an hour.'

'Oh, well, then maybe we're not there yet.' That kept everyone quiet for a while. Mind you, you can tell when you're finally 'there' when you see the grown-ups tumble out of the car and go as far away as they can from the kids who've tormented them for all those hours. So once and for all, please note: if mum and dad are still near enough to answer your question, then the answer is: no. You're not there yet.

31 What is Ben doing in the first paragraph?

A explaining his poor behaviour when travelling
B revealing his dislike of lengthy car journeys
C giving an example of a source of annoyance on trips
D describing a strategy to make journeys pass quickly

32 What is Ben's attitude to the activities he does during the journey?

A He regards them as a bit of a waste of time.
B He regrets that they distract him from the views outside.
C He admits they are not ones he would enjoy doing at home.
D He takes advantage of being free from other obligations.

33 How does Ben behave towards his younger brother Tim during a journey?

A He overreacts to trivial things that Tim does.
B He deliberately encourages Tim to continue to fight.
C He places the blame for any arguments on Tim.
D He tricks Tim into misbehaving.

34 What does 'This' refer to in line 43?

A the speed of the car
B the adults' response
C the fight
D Tim's behaviour

35 What does 'he's got me on a technicality' mean in lines 53 and 54?

A He has taken pleasure in Ben's discomfort.
B He has used the rules to defeat Ben.
C He has managed to spoil Ben's journey.
D He has realised what has annoyed Ben.

36 In the final paragraph, Ben reveals his

A lack of understanding of his dad's sense of humour.
B sympathy for what his parents have endured.
C concern that he has pushed his parents too far.
D resentment at his parents' wish to distance themselves.

Part 6

You are going to read a newspaper article about listening to birdsong. Six sentences have been removed from the article. Choose from the sentences **A–G** the one which fits each gap (**37–42**). There is one extra sentence which you do not need to use.

Mark your answers **on the separate answer sheet.**

The importance of birdsong

Do you enjoy listening to birdsong and, if so, how often do you *really* listen to it? One of the pleasures I share with my grandfather is a love of birds, and in particular listening to their different songs. Some people who hear a bird singing say 'That sounds lovely', without feeling any need to identify the bird in question. Others, including dedicated bird-watchers, will hear the song and immediately set about trying to identify the bird. **37** ______ After all, the next interesting species is sure to turn up soon. My grandfather takes yet another approach.

Recently we made a plan. We decided that once a week or so, we'd go down to the wetlands near where we live, take a hot drink and sit and listen to a species of bird called the sedge warbler. Out on empty wetlands, you can't help but hear these creatures. We don't concern ourselves with whether they're male or female, or what exactly they're doing. **38** ______ Although they may not sing as beautifully as some other birds, they're still worth paying attention to.

In fact, if you look at a scientific analysis of their song, you find that they sing for an entire minute without stopping, and in that time, they will utter around 300 syllables. **39** ______ They will introduce up to ten new syllables in that section. And some analysts say that the music they make is so intricate that they never sing the same song twice.

However, actually being able to hear birdsong is becoming more of a challenge these days as the air is increasingly filled with the noise of machines and traffic. **40** ______ But then we also risk missing natural sounds, and those, it seems, are important for our well-being. Studies have shown that exposure to white noise negatively affects our concentration and stress levels.

Listening to birdsong is the perfect antidote. Recent research has shown what many of us have always thought. **41** ______ There's also evidence that it can lead to a reduction in anxiety levels, particularly useful in hospital environments, for example. These benefits have also been recognised in locations such as airports. One airport has started to play birdsong to passengers in its quiet lounge, where people can unwind before flights, and so far, feedback has been very positive.

Birdsong is also a great reminder that despite human activity, much of which can severely affect their habitats, there are entire communities of birds that are thriving – and living independently alongside us. As birds go about their daily business of laying eggs, raising chicks and finding food, they aren't concerned with us in the least. We may be the centre of our own worlds, but we are most certainly not the centre of theirs. **42** ______ Indeed, seeing the world from a non-human perspective helps us to reconnect with nature and enables us to see the bigger picture.

A It provides physical relaxation as well as mental stimulation.

B The objective is rather to listen to the song as another example of how amazing nature can be.

C It can be a key indicator of the health of the bird population.

D The only solution is to wear headphones and block it all out.

E The middle of the song is the most complex.

F That is something we should be more aware of.

G Having done so to their satisfaction, they'll move on.

Part 7

You are going to read an article about some young film directors. For questions **43–52**, choose from the people (**A–D**). The people may be chosen more than once.

Mark your answers **on the separate answer sheet.**

Which person

describes the opportunity they were given to analyse challenging films?	**43**	
admits their approach wasn't typical of the way new directors tend to behave?	**44**	
believes that it is necessary to change the subject matter of their films regularly?	**45**	
mentions the challenging environment they had to work in?	**46**	
says that they don't want to criticise filmmakers in a different working environment?	**47**	
admits they had difficulty mastering one skill required for their work?	**48**	
describes a technique that they use to create a particular atmosphere in their films?	**49**	
explains how they aren't limited by certain demands that other filmmakers have to meet?	**50**	
enjoys writing about complex personalities that may not be easy to like?	**51**	
mentions how the actors need to feel committed to what they are doing?	**52**	

Young film directors

A Laurence Yuen

My main task is to come up with a narrative that everyone finds engaging. It's all down to the quality of that story because, if a director isn't working in Hollywood or somewhere like that, there might not be the budget to pay the cast what they deserve. This means they all need to believe passionately in the story that's being told and want to come to work every day despite the lack of financial reward. I'd never knock people employed by the big studios because some fantastic films are made there, but independent filmmakers like me have greater freedom, so we can tell more unusual stories without worrying too much about the need to make money or please huge audiences. For example, I like creating characters that are different from what you might typically see in big Hollywood movies and which don't always conform to stereotypes.

B Daisy Morgan

I didn't start out with an interest in making animated films, but I gradually realised there was potential in that field. I struggled initially and it took me a good six months to get the hang of it. When most directors make their first animated feature film, they keep things fairly modest. I didn't scale back or limit my ambition even though we ended up having to do the filming in a confined space – it was really cramped. A vital part of the process of writing a film is finding someone to do it with – someone who on a basic level you're compatible with, but doesn't have exactly the same way of doing things. What almost defeated me was the writing, actually. My first few drafts were too long and needed a huge amount of editing, which was hard to take because very promising material had to be cut.

C Antonio Rossi

As a teenager, I'd watch teen movies and then I'd get fed up and, with my parents' encouragement, would watch some of their movies as well and discuss them in detail. This exposed me to complex, sophisticated filmmaking at an early age. Some directors choose to limit themselves to particular themes because it brings them success and popularity. But I try to shake things up when I can – it's the only way to improve, I think. Attending film festivals is a great way of getting direct audience feedback on your work, but having said that, I try not to worry too much if people react negatively towards my films. If I do that, then it starts to block my creativity. I'd love to write a comedy and I thought at one time it might be an easy option. It's not difficult to write what you personally find funny, but trying to write something that everyone else will find equally amusing is a different thing completely.

D Anna Svensson

I prefer writing and directing drama because it gives me the opportunity to create characters full of contradictions – characters that audiences won't necessarily warm to. I often include scenes without dialogue, which adds to the tension and suspense. I love the opportunity to create strong emotional responses in people, particularly by unexpectedly changing the way the viewer feels about a character. Getting hold of the best cameras and lighting is a challenge when you haven't got a huge budget. Trying to decide on what camera to use is sometimes a bit tricky too. We've found that with an inexperienced cast bigger cameras can be off-putting and intrusive. Several top directors may have influenced my work, and I don't think you can hide that from anyone. In the early days I may have stolen some ideas from them, but I didn't see that I was doing it. Even so, it's a bit embarrassing when I look back at my first attempts at filmmaking.

WRITING (1 hour 20 minutes)

Part 1

You **must** answer this question. Write your answer in **140–190** words in an appropriate style on **the separate answer sheet**.

---

1 In your English class you have been talking about schools. Now your English teacher has asked you to write an essay for homework.

Write your essay using **all** the notes and giving reasons for your point of view.

Some people say that schools will be very different in the future.

What do you think?

Notes

Write about:

1. the teachers
2. the subjects
3. .... (your own idea)

Part 2

Write an answer to **one** of the questions **2–4** in this part. Write your answer in **140–190** words in an appropriate style **on the separate answer sheet**. Put the question number in the box at the top of the answer sheet.

---

2 You see this announcement in an international e-magazine for teenagers:

> *Articles wanted*
>
> **The Weather!**
>
> What is your favourite kind of weather and what kind of weather do you hate? Why? What effect does different weather have on your mood?
>
> The best articles will appear online next week.

Write your **article**.

3 You recently saw this notice in an English magazine:

> *Reviews wanted*
>
> **Family-friendly restaurants**
>
> Do you know a restaurant which is especially good for families with children of different ages? If so, write a review describing the restaurant, explaining what kind of food it serves and saying why it is a good restaurant for the whole family.
>
> We will post the best reviews on our website.

Write your **review**.

4 You have received this email from your English friend, Arthur:

> Hi!
>
> My older brother, Stan, is going to your country next year to study. He wants to find out if there are any customs or traditions he should know about. Also, he's not sure whether to live in an apartment on his own or to live with a local family. Which would be best and why?
>
> Thanks
>
> Arthur

Write your **email**.

LISTENING (approximately 40 minutes)

Part 1

You will hear people talking in eight different situations.

For questions **1–8**, choose the best answer (**A**, **B** or **C**).

---

1 You hear two friends talking about a pop band they saw on TV.

What surprised them both about the band members?

A the wide range of ages

B their level of popularity

C the quality of their voices

2 You hear part of an interview with a scientist.

What is he doing?

A explaining why some research has produced unclear results

B criticising the reluctance of some schools to co-operate with him

C pointing out the possible value of making some controversial changes

3 You hear a teacher talking to a student about doing homework.

What advice does she give?

A Take regular short breaks.

B Deal with the difficult things first.

C Cut down on free-time activities.

4 You hear a football fan talking about his team.

He blames their poor results on

A their struggle to maintain energy levels.

B their poor organisation on the pitch.

C their lack of belief in themselves.

5 You hear a film critic talking about a film for teenagers.

What does she say about it?

A She was impressed by the special effects.

B It was better than the book it was based on.

C The actor who played the leading role performed well.

6 You hear two teenagers discussing a visit to a zoo.

They agree that zoos

A attract tourists in imaginative ways.

B can succeed in educating people.

C play a valuable role in conservation.

7 You hear a young professional ballet dancer talking about performing.

What does she say about being on stage?

A She tries to forget any critical comments she's heard.

B She succeeds by pretending to be confident.

C She reveals a very different side of herself.

8 You hear a teacher talking about the history of the refrigerator.

What does he say about it?

A Its introduction caused a great deal of excitement.

B Its potential wasn't recognised for some time.

C Its long-term significance has been overestimated.

Part 2

You will hear a man called Jack Morton talking about his job as a windsurfing instructor. For questions **9–18**, complete the sentences with a word or short phrase.

Jack Morton – windsurfing instructor

Jack's first experience of work was as a **(9)** ....

The name of the first watersports company that Jack worked for was **(10)** ....

What particularly attracts Jack to windsurfing is the **(11)** .... involved.

Jack most enjoys the moment when his beginners learn to **(12)** .... on the board successfully.

Jack uses the word **(13)** .... to describe how some learners feel when they succeed.

Jack explains that getting enough **(14)** .... is more important than anything else when learning to windsurf.

Jack feels that the **(15)** .... is something many windsurfers fail to think carefully about.

Jack mentions parking a car to explain that people should give each other **(16)** .... when windsurfing.

The fact that he is **(17)** .... has earned Jack praise from his employer.

Jack says that **(18)** .... as well as promotional skills are becoming more important in watersports careers.

Part 3

You will hear five short extracts in which teenagers are remembering the day they met their best friend for the first time. For questions **19–23**, choose from the list (**A–H**) how each speaker felt on that day. Use the letters only once. There are three extra letters which you do not need to use.

A disappointed by something the friend said

B pleased to find they shared an interest

C embarrassed by a misunderstanding

D surprised that they hadn't met previously

E happy about a suggestion the friend made

F amused by something they saw together

G nervous about what they had to do together

H curious about the friend's experiences

Speaker 1		**19**
Speaker 2		**20**
Speaker 3		**21**
Speaker 4		**22**
Speaker 5		**23**

Part 4

You will hear an interview with a young artist called Martin Gold, who is learning how to draw the cartoon stories that appear in magazines. For questions **24–30**, choose the best answer (**A**, **B** or **C**).

---

24 What attracted Martin to drawing cartoons?

A his wish to demonstrate his originality

B his fascination with reading comics

C his interest in the techniques involved

25 Martin's school teacher reacted to his choice of career by warning him that

A she couldn't help him to get work experience.

B it would be very hard to find a secure job.

C he might need to consider an alternative to it.

26 Martin continued to follow his ambition because of

A the surprising popularity of his artwork.

B the confidence he had in his own abilities.

C the encouraging responses he'd received from magazines.

27 How did visiting Barcelona help Martin?

A He received help developing his drawing techniques.

B He felt inspired by his experiences there.

C He realised what he really liked about art.

28 By using a different kind of ink for drawing his cartoons, Martin

A increased the amount he was able to produce.

B included a greater degree of detail.

C extended the range of images he can draw.

29 How does Martin feel about his work as a 'ghost artist'?

A It's proving a less valuable experience than he'd hoped.

B It's preventing him from developing his own cartoons.

C It isn't regular enough for him to rely on financially.

30 Martin thinks that he might have problems working as a cartoonist because of

A his tendency to take on too many challenges.

B his reluctance to accept advice from others.

C his disorganised approach to his work.

SPEAKING (14 minutes)

You take the Speaking test with another candidate (possibly two candidates), referred to here as your partner. There are two examiners. One will speak to you and your partner and the other will be listening. Both examiners will award marks.

Part 1 (2 minutes (3 minutes for groups of three))

The examiner asks you and your partner questions about yourselves. You may be asked about things like 'your home town', 'your interests', 'your career plans', etc.

Part 2 (4 minutes (6 minutes for groups of three))

The examiner gives you two photographs and asks you to talk about them for one minute.
The examiner then asks your partner a question about your photographs and your partner responds briefly.
Then the examiner gives your partner two different photographs. Your partner talks about these photographs for one minute. This time the examiner asks you a question about your partner's photographs and you respond briefly.

Part 3 (4 minutes (5 minutes for groups of three))

The examiner asks you and your partner to talk together. They give you a task to look at so you can think about and discuss an idea, giving reasons for your opinion. For example, you may be asked to think about some changes in the world, or about spending free time with your family. After you have discussed the task for about two minutes with your partner, the examiner will ask you a follow-up question, which you should discuss for a further minute.

Part 4 (4 minutes (6 minutes for groups of three))

The examiner asks some further questions, which leads to a more general discussion of what you have talked about in Part 3. You may comment on your partner's answers if you wish.

CAMBRIDGE ENGLISH
Language Assessment
Part of the University of Cambridge

Do not write in this box

SAMPLE

Candidate Name
If not already printed, write name in CAPITALS and complete the Candidate No. grid (in pencil).

Candidate Signature

Examination Title

Centre

Supervisor:
If the candidate is ABSENT or has WITHDRAWN shade here

Centre No.

Candidate No.

Examination Details

0	0	0	0
1	1	1	1
2	2	2	2
3	3	3	3
4	4	4	4
5	5	5	5
6	6	6	6
7	7	7	7
8	8	8	8
9	9	9	9

Candidate Answer Sheet

Instructions

Use a PENCIL (B or HB).

Rub out any answer you wish to change using an eraser.

Parts 1, 5, 6 and 7:
Mark ONE letter for each question.

For example, if you think **B** is the right answer to the question, mark your answer sheet like this:

0	A	B	C	D

Parts 2, 3 and 4:
Write your answer clearly in CAPITAL LETTERS.

For Parts 2 and 3 write one letter in each box. For example:

0	E	X	A	M	P	L	E

Part 1

1	A	B	C	D
2	A	B	C	D
3	A	B	C	D
4	A	B	C	D
5	A	B	C	D
6	A	B	C	D
7	A	B	C	D
8	A	B	C	D

Part 2

		Do not write below here
9		9 1 0 u
10		10 1 0 u
11		11 1 0 u
12		12 1 0 u
13		13 1 0 u
14		14 1 0 u
15		15 1 0 u
16		16 1 0 u

Continues over →

Part 3

		Do not write below here
17		17 1 0 u
18		18 1 0 u
19		19 1 0 u
20		20 1 0 u
21		21 1 0 u
22		22 1 0 u
23		23 1 0 u
24		24 1 0 u

Part 4

		Do not write below here
25		25 2 1 0 u
26		26 2 1 0 u
27		27 2 1 0 u
28		28 2 1 0 u
29		29 2 1 0 u
30		30 2 1 0 u

Part 5

31	A	B	C	D
32	A	B	C	D
33	A	B	C	D
34	A	B	C	D
35	A	B	C	D
36	A	B	C	D

Part 6

37	A	B	C	D	E	F	G
38	A	B	C	D	E	F	G
39	A	B	C	D	E	F	G
40	A	B	C	D	E	F	G
41	A	B	C	D	E	F	G
42	A	B	C	D	E	F	G

Part 7

43	A	B	C	D	E	F
44	A	B	C	D	E	F
45	A	B	C	D	E	F
46	A	B	C	D	E	F
47	A	B	C	D	E	F
48	A	B	C	D	E	F
49	A	B	C	D	E	F
50	A	B	C	D	E	F
51	A	B	C	D	E	F
52	A	B	C	D	E	F

CAMBRIDGE ENGLISH
Language Assessment
Part of the University of Cambridge

Do not write in this box

SAMPLE

Candidate Name
If not already printed, write name in CAPITALS and complete the Candidate No. grid (in pencil).

Candidate Signature

Examination Title

Centre

Supervisor:
If the candidate is ABSENT or has WITHDRAWN shade here

Centre No.

Candidate No.

Examination Details

0	0	0	0
1	1	1	1
2	2	2	2
3	3	3	3
4	4	4	4
5	5	5	5
6	6	6	6
7	7	7	7
8	8	8	8
9	9	9	9

Candidate Answer Sheet

Instructions

Use a PENCIL (B or HB).
Rub out any answer you wish to change using an eraser.

Parts 1, 3 and **4:**
Mark ONE letter for each question.

For example, if you think **B** is the right answer to the question, mark your answer sheet like this:

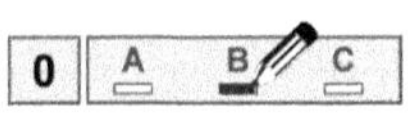

Part 2:
Write your answer clearly in CAPITAL LETTERS.

Write one letter or number in each box.
If the answer has more than one word, leave one box empty between words.

For example:

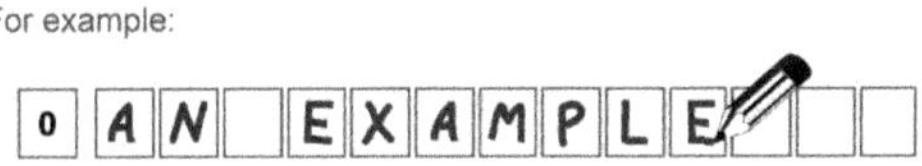

Turn this sheet over to start.

Part 1

1	A	B	C
2	A	B	C
3	A	B	C
4	A	B	C
5	A	B	C
6	A	B	C
7	A	B	C
8	A	B	C

Part 2 (Remember to write in CAPITAL LETTERS or numbers)

		Do not write below here
9		9 1 0 u
10		10 1 0 u
11		11 1 0 u
12		12 1 0 u
13		13 1 0 u
14		14 1 0 u
15		15 1 0 u
16		16 1 0 u
17		17 1 0 u
18		18 1 0 u

Part 3

19	A	B	C	D	E	F	G	H
20	A	B	C	D	E	F	G	H
21	A	B	C	D	E	F	G	H
22	A	B	C	D	E	F	G	H
23	A	B	C	D	E	F	G	H

Part 4

24	A	B	C
25	A	B	C
26	A	B	C
27	A	B	C
28	A	B	C
29	A	B	C
30	A	B	C

Acknowledgements

The authors and publishers acknowledge the following sources of copyright material and are grateful for the permissions granted. While every effort has been made, it has not always been possible to identify the sources of all the material used, or to trace all copyright holders. If any omissions are brought to our notice, we will be happy to include the appropriate acknowledgements on reprinting and in the next update to the digital edition, as applicable.

Key: B = Below, T = Top.

Text

Dogo Media Inc. for the text on p. 10 adapted from 'Scientists Confirm That In Order To Succeed, You Have To First Fail' by Avery Elizabeth Hurt, 09.12.2014. Copyright © 2014 Dogo Media Inc. Reproduced with permission; Guardian News & Media Ltd. for the text on p. 14 adapted from 'An author at 15: teenage girls had to be ugly, naive or antisocial' by Kate Kellaway, *The Guardian*, 01.02.2015. Copyright © 2015 Guardian News & Media Ltd. Reproduced with permission; Guardian News & Media Ltd. for the text on adapted p. 16 from 'Swedish school sheds light on dark days on winter' by David Crouch, *The Guardian*, 24.01.2015. Copyright © 2015 Guardian News & Media Ltd. Reproduced with permission; New York Daily News for the text on p.33 adapted from "New Yorkers encouraged to 'act like a kid' and jump on bed in middle of city" by Joel Landau, Daily News, 02.12.2014. Copyright © 2014 New York Daily News. Reproduced with permission; Los Angeles Times for the text on p. 36 from 'Teens Launch Balloons To Edge Of Space, And So The Adventure Begins' by Deborah Netburn, Los Angeles Times, 17.06.2014. Copyright © 2014 Los Angeles Times. Reproduced with permission; Dogo Media Inc. for the text on p. 38 adapted from 'Crafty Seals Seek Follow Tracking Device Signals To Catch Fish' by Meera Dolasla, 20.11.2014. Copyright © 2014 Dogo Media Inc. Reproduced with permission; The Washington Post for the text on p. 60 from 'Scientists have discovered a new taste that could profoundly change the way we meet' by Roberto A. Ferdman, *The Washington Post*. Copyright © 2017 The Washington Post. Reproduced with permission; NBCUniversal Archives for the text on p. 80 from 'Family road trips: Getting there is not half the fun' by Eric Ruhlater, 15.11.2012. Copyright © 2012 NBCUniversal Archives. Reproduced with permission; Dogo Media Inc. for the text on p. 136 adapted from 'Scientists Discover Spectacular Ruby-Red Seadragon' by Allegra Staples, 26.02.2015. Copyright © 2015 Dogo Media Inc. Reproduced with permission.

Photos

All photographs are sourced from Getty Images.

p. C1 (T): Hill Street Studios/Blend Images; p. C1 (B), p. C5 (B), p. C10 (T): Hero Images; p. C2 (T): Sean De Burca/The Image Bank; p. C2 (B), p. C4 (T): Steve Debenport/E+; p. C4 (B), p. C7 (T): asiseeit/E+; p. C5 (T): Sam Edwards/Caiaimage; p. C7 (B): Robert Daly/Caiaimage; p. C8 (T): Emir Memedovski/E+; p. C8 (B): MivPiv/ E+; p. C10 (B): Hero Images/DigitalVision; p. C11 (T): Christa Paustenbaugh Photography/Moment Open; p. C11 (B): PeopleImages/E+.

Visual materials for the Speaking test

What are the people enjoying about doing these activities in after school clubs?

1A

1B

Why have the people decided to take photographs in these situations?

1C

1D

1E

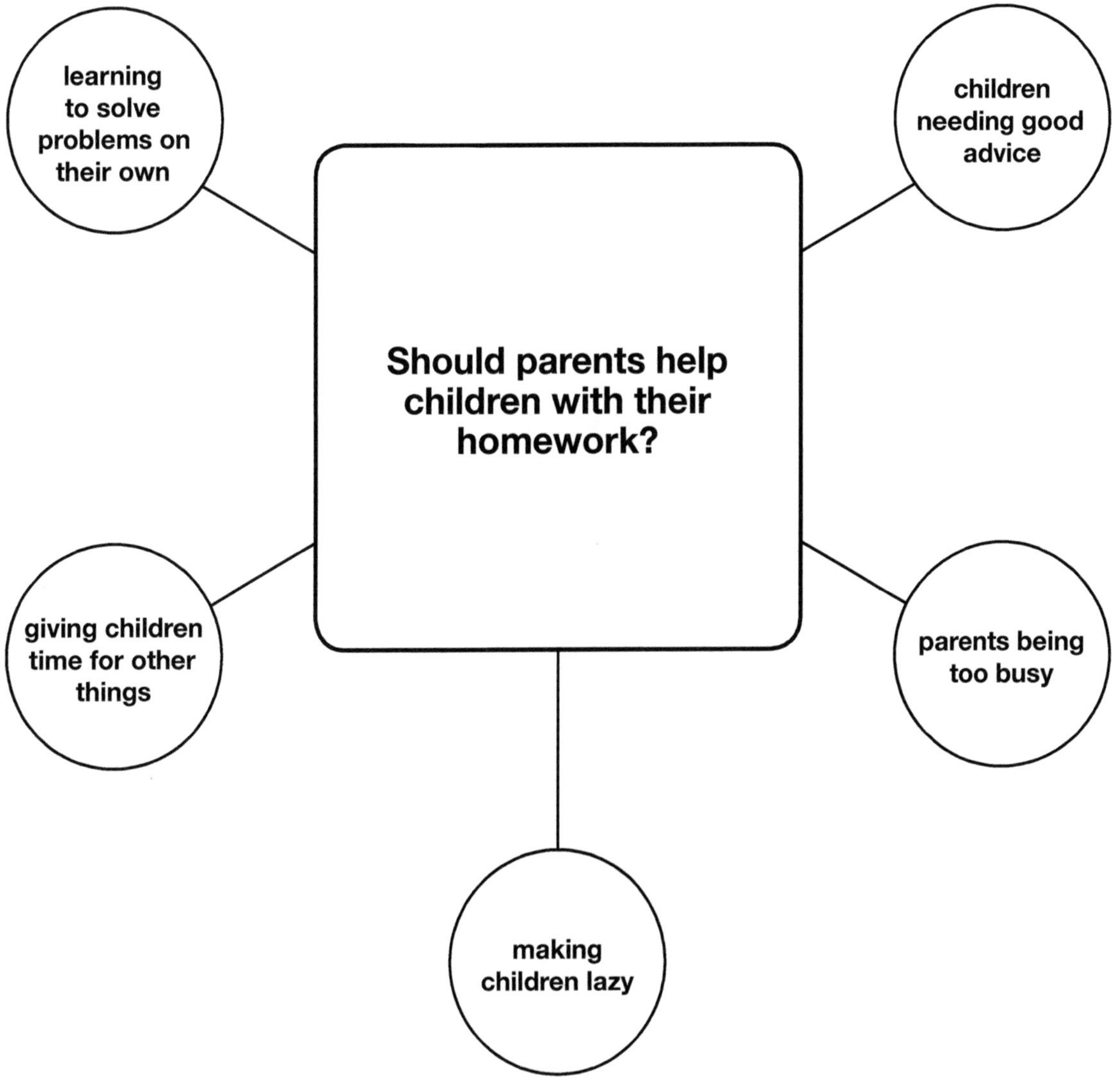
Should parents help children with their homework?
learning to solve problems on their own
children needing good advice
giving children time for other things
parents being too busy
making children lazy

Why are the people listening carefully in these situations?

2A

2B

What are the families enjoying about spending their holidays in these places?

2C

2D

2E

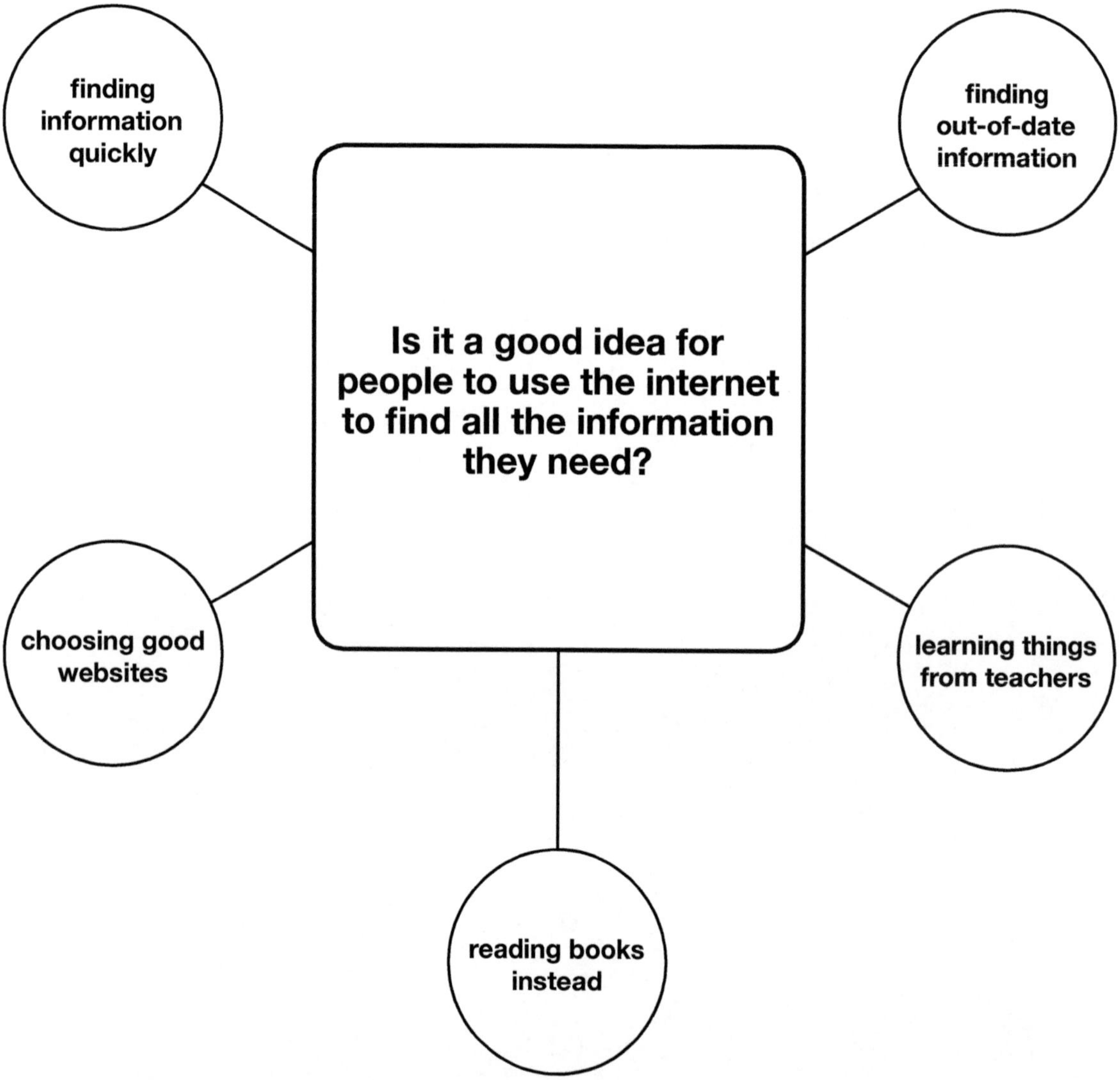
Is it a good idea for people to use the internet to find all the information they need?
finding information quickly
finding out-of-date information
choosing good websites
learning things from teachers
reading books instead

Why are the people working together in these situations?

3A

3B

What is difficult for the people about learning these things?

3C

3D

3E

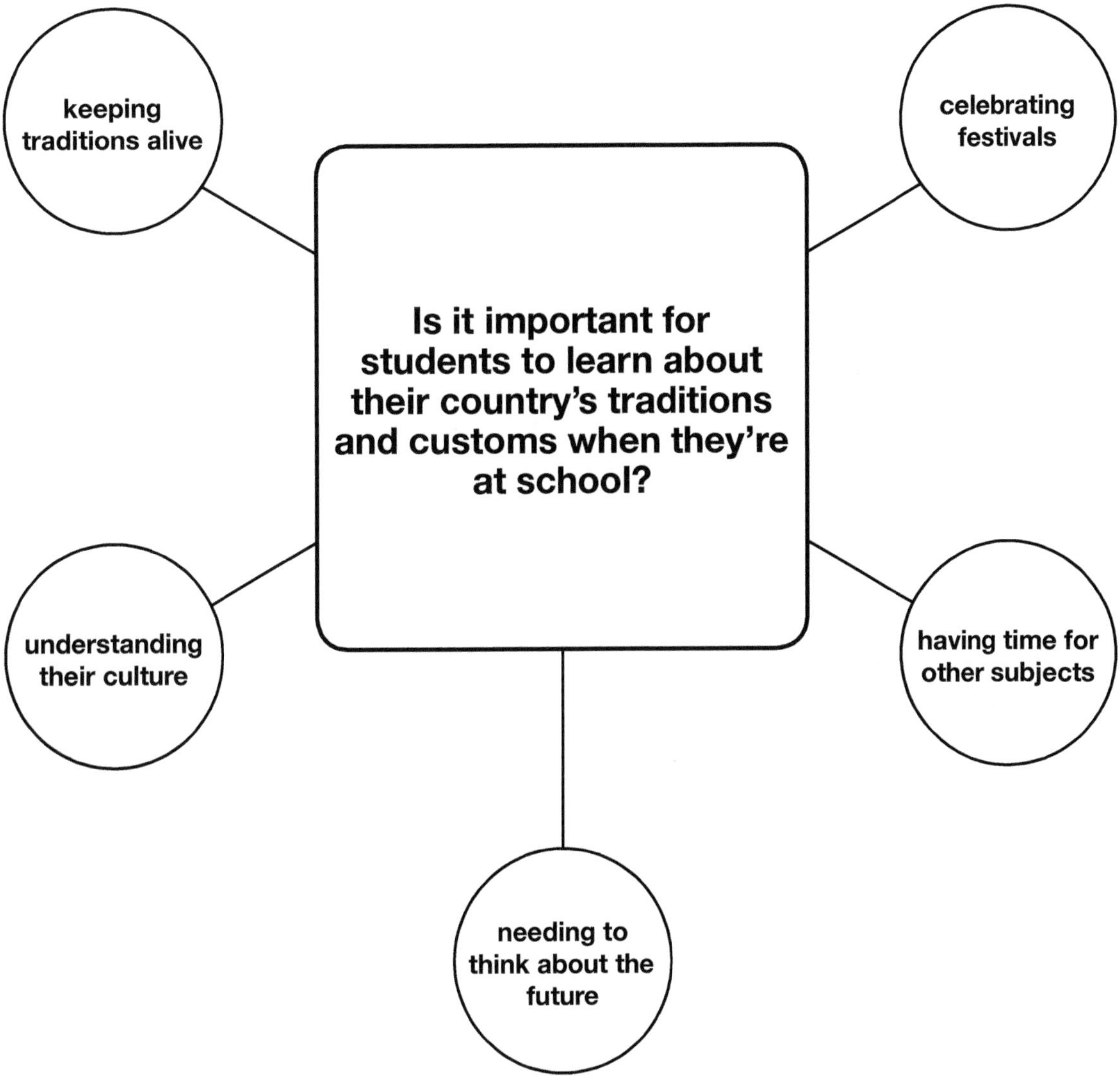
Is it important for students to learn about their country's traditions and customs when they're at school?
keeping traditions alive
celebrating festivals
understanding their culture
having time for other subjects
needing to think about the future

What are the advantages of studying science in these ways?

4A

4B

Why have these people decided to spend time on their own?

4C

4D

4E

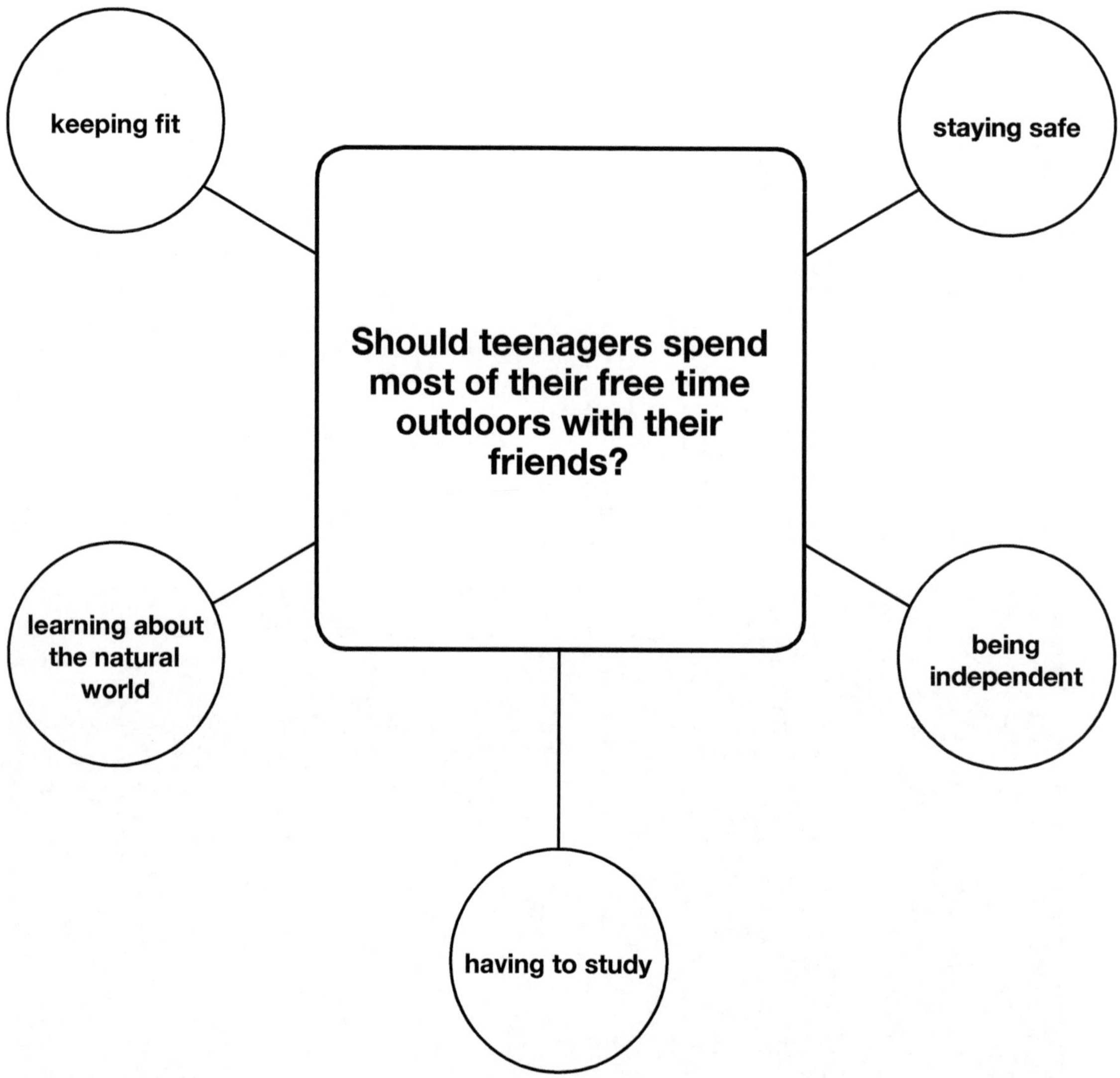
Should teenagers spend most of their free time outdoors with their friends?
keeping fit
staying safe
learning about the natural world
being independent
having to study

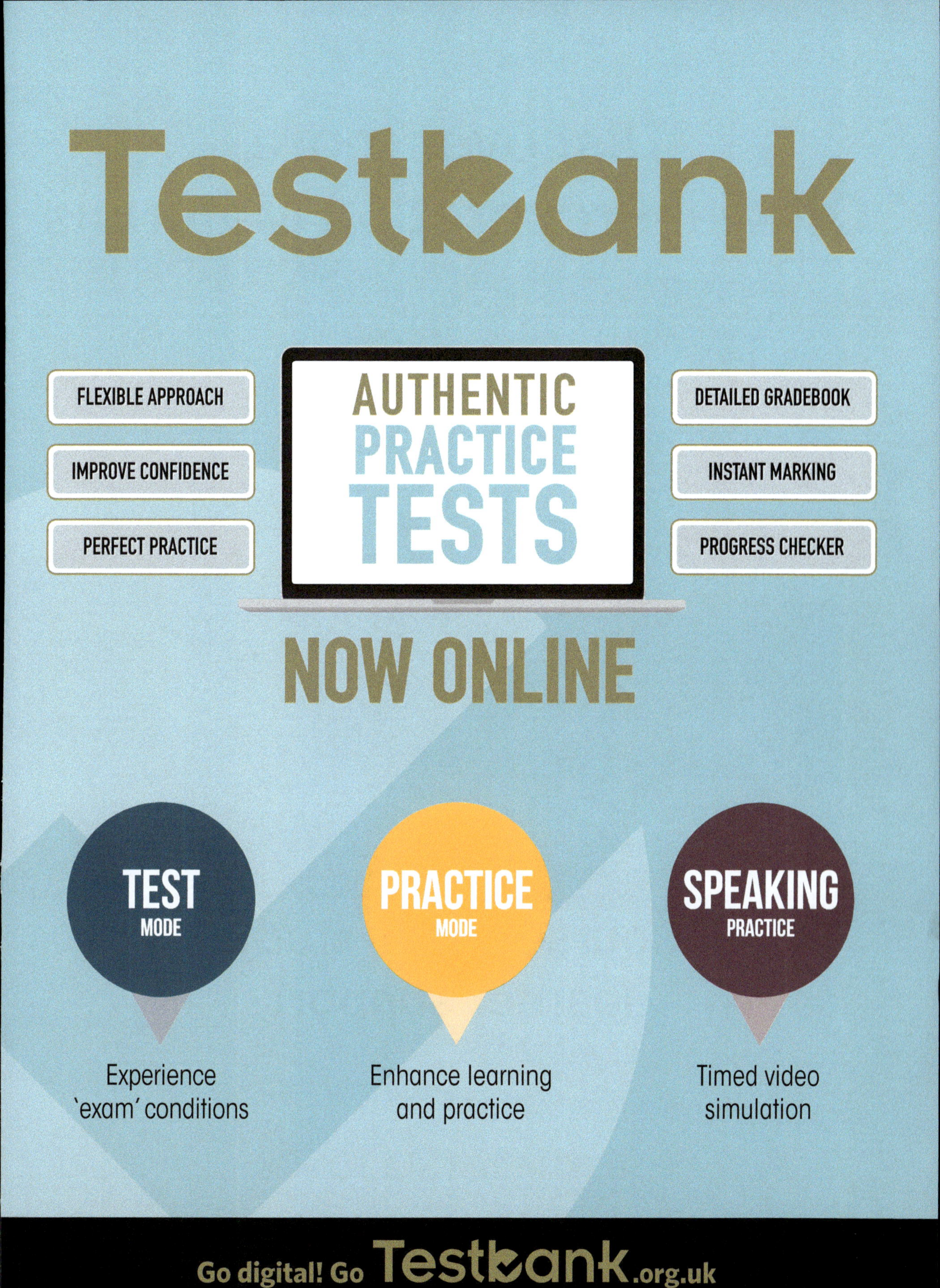
Testbank
FLEXIBLE APPROACH
IMPROVE CONFIDENCE
PERFECT PRACTICE
AUTHENTIC PRACTICE TESTS
DETAILED GRADEBOOK
INSTANT MARKING
PROGRESS CHECKER
NOW ONLINE
TEST MODE
Experience 'exam' conditions
PRACTICE MODE
Enhance learning and practice
SPEAKING PRACTICE
Timed video simulation
Go digital! Go Testbank.org.uk